T0301242

Chinese and
Any Other Asian

Dr Anna Sulan Masing is an academic, poet and journalist. She co-founded SOURCED, a public research platform that explores our global food and drink systems, and is co-founder and editor-in-chief of *Cheese* magazine. Anna Sulan's ten-part narrative podcast, *Taste of Place*, by Whetstone Radio Collective, explores colonialism and nostalgia through the history of pepper.

Anna Sulan has written for various publications, including BBC Travel World's Table, CNN, the *Guardian*, *Foodism*, *Good Beer Hunting*, *Waitrose Food* and *Apartamento*. Her work has been shortlisted at the Guild of Food Writers and Fortnum & Mason Food Awards. She has spoken at various symposiums around the world on the topic of drinks, sustainability, heritage, gender and identity.

Anna Sulan's doctorate investigated storytelling practices of the Iban, a South East Asian Indigenous peoples of which she is part of. It explored how those practices migrated, and how identity changes when space and location changes. This looked at the intersection of performance, gender, farming practices and identity.

Chinese and
Any Other Asian

*Exploring East and South East
Asian Identity in Britain*

ANNA SULAN MASING

WEIDENFELD & NICOLSON

First published in Great Britain in 2025 by Weidenfeld & Nicolson,
an imprint of The Orion Publishing Group Ltd
Carmelite House, 50 Victoria Embankment
London EC4Y 0DZ

An Hachette UK Company

The authorised representative in the EEA is Hachette Ireland,
8 Castlecourt Centre, Dublin 15, D15 XTP3,
Ireland (email: info@hbgi.ie)

1 3 5 7 9 10 8 6 4 2

A CIP catalogue record for this book is
available from the British Library.

ISBN (Hardback) 978 1 3996 0665 3
ISBN (Ebook) 978 1 3996 0667 7
ISBN (Audio) 978 1 3996 0668 4

Typeset at The Spartan Press Ltd,
Lymington, Hants

Printed in Great Britain by Clays Ltd,
Elcograf S.p.A.

www.weidenfeldandnicolson.co.uk
www.orionbooks.co.uk

To
James Jemut Masing
and
Fiona Frances Mowlem;
my heroes, my beginning.

Contents

Introduction

Borders and Beginnings

One summer I was coming home to the UK from a holiday in Europe. The woman at immigration asked me why I was travelling by myself; baffled, I explained my husband at the time was staying on longer. She told me I couldn't travel alone.

'So women can't travel without their husbands?' I asked.

'Not with your visa,' she said, looking at my spousal visa in my New Zealand passport.

'I have the power to detain you,' she emphasised.

'Well, detain me then,' I said, with calm fury.

She let me through, explaining I was lucky she was in a good mood.

Once, after I'd obtained my British passport, an immigration officer at the UK border asked why I was born outside of the UK. She questioned the legitimacy of my having a British passport. 'Where were you born? Where is Woden Valley? Yes, I can see it is on your passport, but why? Are you sure it is in Australia? Why do you have a UK passport?'

She eventually let me pass. I have yet to hear a white

friend with similar passports or visas have the same conversations. I only ever use the electronic machines now, regardless of the queues.

When sitting my Life in the UK test, to prove I was British enough to deserve the citizenship, I remember having to answer the question, 'What is the significance of 14 February?' I also remember the way the test facilitators spoke to all of us who were taking the test in a dark basement room in Islington. It was condescending, with hard voices, and no room for questions. It was clear the idea was to intimidate.

My identity, my non-whiteness, my Asian-ness performs difference at borders. Borders are found in so many places in the UK, not just in the immigration queue at Gatwick Airport. Throughout my life here I have felt both welcomed and found home, but I have also been marginalised and shut out, or asked to perform belonging in what has felt like ritualistic dances. Yes, I've read *1984*, know how to pour a pint, can name the six wives of Henry VIII, and have an opinion about whether it's jam or cream first on a scone (cream, it acts like butter).

I came to the UK to study, leaving New Zealand on my twentieth birthday, and never left. In this country I have earnt an undergraduate degree and a PhD. I bought a small flat, pledged my allegiance to the Queen and lived with people from all over the world. I've worked in bars and restaurants, in a law firm, and in the fashion industry. I was a sub-editor for *The Times*, founded and ran a theatre company, a small communications agency, and launched a print magazine. I've eaten, drank, laughed, cried, paid taxes, travelled Europe. My belonging in this country is multifaceted, and is part of so many others' stories. I am anchored here by all of these things. This is my home.

But when I filled in the 2021 census, my options on ethnic identity under 'Mixed or Multiple ethnic groups' were 'White and Asian'. The definition of 'Asian' in the census is: 'Indian', 'Pakistani', 'Bangladeshi', 'Chinese' or 'Any other Asian background'. Under the category of 'White' is: 'English, Welsh, Scottish, Northern Irish or British', 'Irish', 'Gypsy or Irish Traveller', 'Roma' or 'Any other White background'. There are no Chinese Scottish, Vietnamese Welsh or Mixed Irish identities available. Non-white identities have no additional cultural or national nuance. We have no ties to a region or spatial relatability; we don't have a place to belong to. And the act of ticking 'other', which so many of us are made to do, is an act of othering, and we are having to do it to ourselves because the society we live in does not recognise us. It is dehumanising. It is saying there is a norm that we don't fit. It isn't just the census – medical forms, job applications, the National Insurance number application and more all ask us to define ourselves in this limited way. Bureaucracy eradicates our belonging. We are illegitimate in the borders of society, and this has lasting and devastating effects.

That is why I am writing this book.

Chinese and Any Other Asian explores the identity of

people with East and South East Asian heritage, backgrounds and culture, and we are so much more complex and complicated than Chinese, or Any Other Asian. Ticking a box on a form seems mindless and small, a throwaway moment that doesn't matter in everyday life, but throughout this book I untangle the damaging consequences of the limiting, condensing and shrinking of our identity into this category.

During the Covid-19 pandemic there was a rise in hate and violence against those of East, or perceived East, Asian heritage. This racism didn't emerge from a vacuum. The cultural, political and bureaucratical landscape of Britain led to this. How did we get here?

This book is my love letter to people I have met and the place I call home. I weave history with personal narrative, and I speak to people throughout the UK who have a variety of different heritages and belongings to East and South East Asia. I explore the many journeys of how we got to Britain and hope to paint a picture of a vast set of identities of those with East and South East Asian histories. For every person I have spoken to, and story I tell, there are hundreds not told, and there are hundreds of details from each story that I could not fit into these pages. To understand the depth of racism that the community has experienced is, and has been, very painful and I am immensely grateful to everyone who has shared their stories and thoughts. In the last few years, there has been a growing recognition of an identity, a collective identity, under the acronym 'ESEA' – East and South East Asian – therefore this is a book that also looks to understand the power in community, activism and coming together. What do we mean by solidarity? How do we support each other? These are questions that I have explored.

Chinese and Any Other Asian is a journey for me to try and understand and get to know how Britain's history of colonialism and its migration policies have shaped our society today. I wanted to examine the importance of language and understand how we frame issues around race and the ESEA identities. I also wanted to look at the violence that ESEA people have endured and understand the various ways in which this violence manifests – from physical assault to the language society uses to describe ESEA people. When we look at identity, we have to understand the various intersections we sit at. It is never just about race. Investigating gender allows us to explore how colonialism, class, race, family and history all intersect, and thinking about our foods can help us unpick how we talk about power and reframe our belonging and narratives. Our cultural landscape – our films, theatre, literature – is influenced by global stories as much as British-specific situations, and it has been impossible to talk about our visual representation without reflecting on the US and Hollywood.

Looking at popular culture, which often knows no national borders, is so key in understanding stereotypes and prejudices. In his book *The Yellow Peril: Dr Fu Manchu & the Rise of Chinaphobia*, cultural historian Christopher

Frayling retells a conversation he had with *Orientalism* author Edward Said about popular culture's overlooked impact on the way we think about race. 'Mass media, certainly films, have a much more powerful, simplifying and reductive effect. Because they are *visual*,' said Said.[1]

But it isn't just modern-day media, with countless war films set in South East Asia, that has painted these caricature pictures of peoples. These are narratives built on centuries of exoticism and othering. Frayling points out that in Victorian England, there were many articles and journalist 'investigations' into opium dens in East London. For example, he writes that Charles Dickens' descriptions of opium dens 'had a profound influence on the ways in which such dwellings were described by novelists, storytellers and journalists in the future, and on the public debate about opium smoking: the dark alleyway, the miserable court, the Arabian Nights fantasy, the collapsed bedstead'.[2] The popular media of Victorian England and, later, the portrayal of the villainous Dr Fu Manchu by both novelist Sax Rohmer and countless filmmakers throughout the twentieth century, all echo the language newspapers used in the 1970s and 1980s around monosodium glutamate (a flavour enhancer, commonly known as MSG) in Chinese restaurants. From a brief mention in a letter to the editor of the *New England Journal of Medicine* in the US in 1968, relating to eating at a Chinese restaurant and feeling ill afterwards, media across the US and the UK helped develop a narrative around MSG by labelling it as unhealthy and claiming it was related to a phenomena dubbed 'Chinese restaurant syndrome'. This language conjures images of distrustful migrants, looking to poison the innocent local communities. It was a short step therefore towards the Asian hate of Covid-19.

And so it is within these spaces of storytelling that we get to see how powerful narratives can be, and how this power has been used to cause great danger, violence and othering. But, it is also a place where I see great opportunity for change.

Reductive stories and bureaucratic tick boxes have made identities simplistic. This allows for violence to become acceptable because it dehumanises and brings othering into the everyday. How can we change that lens? How can we find new stories to tell, and develop a cultural landscape away from racism, bias and stereotype? This book is also a moment to sit with various people and listen to their stories, to relish in all the difference and to allow ourselves to be open to hearing more in the future.

East Asia includes China, Japan, Mongolia, North Korea, South Korea and Taiwan. Within these nation states are contested borders and various ways of recognition between places and cultural identities that defy national lines. South East Asia is all places south of mainland China, east of India and north-west of Australia, and includes Singapore, East Timor, Vietnam, Malaysia, Thailand, Cambodia, Brunei, Indonesia, Myanmar, Laos, Philippines; islands and peninsulas bordered mostly by seas and oceans. We are looking at a group of people with heritages from the snowy plains east of Siberia to the tropical jungles in the Indonesian archipelago. And yet here we are, being asked to tick 'Chinese' or 'Any other Asian' on forms.

Where do we begin to explore the identities of East and South East Asian people in Britain? A story has to start somewhere, and this one starts with me.

This story starts with opening a new Word document with a glass of Scotch whisky in hand, on a Sunday afternoon in autumn, in East London. It is that sort of cold outside that could be described as crisp, where humidity is absent and if you stand still for too long the chill seeps deep into your bones, and you can taste the coming Christmas season. Inside, the fading daylight makes me feel that having whisky at 4 p.m. is the most appropriate thing to do as I start a daunting task.

When you're talking about a party, reminiscing to a friend, do you start by explaining the annual ritual of a birthday, the date you received the invitation, or when you arrived at the party? My existence in the UK is not a party, but there are similarities. There are people – friends, strangers, colleagues. There is fun, there is always gossip, there is political chat over drinks and new friends made in bathroom queues at house parties and bars. And you introduce yourself over and over again: explain why you're there, who you are, what you do, and who invited you. Sometimes these interactions are hostile, gatekeeping your access to the space. Sometimes they are welcoming, with curious questions about your story.

I am the product of colonialism, a child of the empire; I am the now that before made happen. There is no version of me that exists in this space of London, of England, of the UK, that isn't informed by the stories of a homeland that I had never been to until I turned twenty. And the fact that English is my 'native language' is not just from my parents, but the language I was taught in a government school in Sarawak, Malaysia from the age of six.

My mother is a white New Zealander, of predominantly Scottish heritage, and my father was Iban, an Indigenous group in Sarawak, a state of Malaysia on the Borneo island. Both are post-colonial spaces, both at some point were a part of the British Empire. I grew up in both spaces, and I also grew up in London.

I feel like I have been writing this book my whole life. But I began the serious part of research and writing it twenty-one days after my father died and one week after I returned to London from attending his funeral in Sarawak. The memory of equator heat was still on my skin. It was twenty-one months after the UK first went into lockdown because of the global pandemic. It was a time when the rest of the world felt both incredibly close as we all continued to face down a virus together, and yet so far away as so many of us had been stranded far from family. Borders had closed down and the multiple concepts of home – be it driving to Wales for Christmas or traversing the globe to Hong Kong, Singapore or Japan to see cousins, siblings and grandparents – were not just difficult and out of reach, but illegal.

The brutality of missing home for so long – the ache of the absence of tropical rain, of tasting laksa, of the smell of the midday sun – and to finally be able to return only to say a goodbye, was a sharp realisation of how much my sense of home, belonging and identity is connected with spaces outside of my chosen home. I have had the privilege, even when being challenged at borders, of travelling the world with little thought other than 'can I afford this plane fare?' (a valid and anxiety-inducing question in its own right, of course).

But the group effort and complex organisation of getting my siblings and I back to Sarawak at that time, from so many of my family and friends, accentuated my understanding of how borders work and are part of my sense of identity. Borders are only able to exist if they are policed, and this policing is a part of and fundamental to our ESEA understanding of belonging and identity in the UK. We are consistently defined by the spaces we are allowed in and on what terms we are allowed in them.

My story is a diasporic one that is about understanding my identity within a community described as East and South East Asian in the UK. It is about discovering the borders of that identity, borders that are fluid and expand-ing but are also, so often, put in place by those not within this community. My story is of finding home, of finding pockets of people to belong with and spaces to thrive in. It's a story that is soaked, lathered and wrapped in the concept of community, where the last twenty years have shown me that connectivity with others who identify as East and/or South East Asian has been a thread that has held my space in London, and the UK, firm.

Choosing a beginning is a big decision. It shapes the rest of the story. I like to see a beginning as an anchor, a place to radiate out from. It should be a point from which we can expand a story and weave multiple threads. It gives room for the narrative to come back to, to loop around and re-examine, and to never be linear. A linear story has the danger of skipping past voices and hiding truths, whereas I want to tell a story that allows for multiplicity and contradictions. It is only in messiness that we can really begin to understand each other.

And so this story also begins twenty years, two months and seventeen days before I opened that Word document, when I arrived in the UK. This story is not a memoir, but I begin with me to find a way through the many stories of those who are part of the East and South East Asian community in the UK – a community that I have found so much solace in, particularly in the last few years. These stories have an arrival narrative, be it yesterday or centuries ago, and they have the activity of building home and belonging in spaces that are othering, spaces that define these stories and the people that speak them as marginalised.

There are of course, many beginnings. One of those is why I am here in the first place. As the late cultural theorist Stuart Hall said, 'They are here because you were there. There is an umbilical connection. There is no understanding Englishness without understanding its imperial and colonial dimensions.'[3]

This book is a beginning because it is also an invitation, a suggestion of what might become. By beginning, I am sending an invitation to others to tell their stories and their own beginnings too.

Chapter 1

Language

Where are you from?

'From my mother's vagina, you asshole,' my friend Lisa X,* a Vietnamese Australian who has now lived in London for thirteen years, wishes she could answer to everyone who asks. Those four words are so succinct in excluding you. When someone who is comfortable in their belongingness asks that question, they are asserting the space as theirs and not yours. You are other, to their norm.

Otherness is where racism sits, curled up in its lap. Waiting to unfurl, to hiss and to bite. Otherness is a concept that confines you to a place of difference that is not celebrated. To feel like you are 'other' is to feel unsafe, to feel like you don't belong, to feel like your value is less than. To 'other' is to dehumanise. That's what those four words can do. Where are you from? *Not here*, is what they are saying.

The West is able to be defined *because* of the other. Do we have whiteness and Blackness if we don't have the other? Do we have the global north, without the

---

* A pseudonym.

historical and continued exploitation of the global south? 'The Orient has helped to define Europe (or the West) as its contrasting image, idea, personality, experience,' Edward Said writes in *Orientalism*.[1]* 'Oriental' was a word I remember as a child, used to describe people from East and South East Asia. Oriental was spoken in place of 'other'. Otherness is an act of violence, dressed up in words. Language is powerful. Stories are told as a way to pass down cultural learnings and reflections of a society, and fairy tales teach you of the norms, warn you of the dangers. Language is so important when discussing racism, identity, home and belonging. And it is also tricky because language shifts and changes, as it should.

I know that I want to break away from the binary, this construct that has been created by the West, of 'other' and the opposite. The Iban stories of my childhood that softly tell of multiple ways of looking at things, of banishing a binary and believing in the spirits in the trees, are the foundations that want me to tear down a sense of the opposite and instead find identity in the multiplicity. So how do we find the language to undo the othering and the binary damage? How do we find the language to articulate the way we feel and show how racial structures

---

* Said explains that the idea of the Orient does shift depending on the lens, such as America having a different perspective because of relationships with 'the far east', such as Japan. As I quote from a 2003 reprint of the 1978 book, we can see the change in time shifts the idea of location and scope of what is 'the orient'.

are damaging or violent? And how do we find a common language to build solidarity?

But before diving into those questions, it feels important to explain a few words and terms I am using throughout this book, and how and why I have chosen to use them. Throughout this book I am explaining the problematic use of words or terms, and explaining how limiting definitions end up excluding and alienating. Through careful use of language, we can move away from otherness, where one day the question 'where are you from?' is a question about journeys and not a static sense of belonging and excluding.

Mixed race

I use this phrase to describe myself. I have had many descriptors used by others to describe my identity – half-caste being the most common growing up. At the time, I didn't think much of it. I knew I was a tale of two halves. But I remember as a child connecting the idea with plaster of Paris, of casting a mould, of making something into a cast. And so that imagined image became connected with me: someone who was only half cast, only half built, only half made. I felt myself walking around the playground as incomplete, without the possibility of becoming whole.

I learnt fairly soon that the words are different (cast and caste) but really, in terms of racialising someone – are they any different? It was adults, particularly schoolteachers, who referred to me as this with no negative intentions; it was just the 1980s in New Zealand. But they still saw me as half of a whole.

I sometimes say I am 'half white' or 'half Iban/ Malaysian', but I feel much messier than a 'half'. I feel like my identity spills out over everything, doesn't easily stay within boundaries. I've grown up in multiple cultural spaces, moved through and lived in many locations and feel both at home and an outsider in all of these places. I want to take control of my identity and not be caught between two places and halves, to have agency and the ability to hold multiple locations and identities in one hand. I want to be messy and complex. This is why I choose 'mixed', because I am mixed, in all the best ways possible. My identity shifts and I have to respond to these shifts.

The other important aspect is to specifically use the word 'race'. Because of the impact of colonialism, our Western space is racialised, and it is important to claim positioning in that framing. I need and want to be recognised as someone who is judged and seen as 'not white', as being given a racial identity and all the baggage and difficulty that comes with that. Some people may be read as white who are of mixed or multiple (non-white) heritage, but their experience is still racialised as they navigate their relationship with their parents, their histories, their experiences and the world around them.

Journalist and editor Suyin Haynes, who is Chinese

Malaysian and white British, tells me that, although she is not often racialised as East or South East Asian, she has been brought up with a strong sense of her Chinese Malaysian heritage. 'My grandfather was Hakka and they were known for being a nomadic people, and my grandfather was so agitated and ready to get out of his village in the 1950s, and walk on foot to Guangzhou [a couple of days' journey], to get on a boat to Malaysia. And then you [Suyin points to her mother, Linda] grew up in Penang, then moved to the UK, and then I moved to Hong Kong temporarily ... we all have the spirit of moving around,' Suyin explains. This sense of identity, this sense of movement due to a cultural heritage, is very much a part of Suyin's identity.

In Naomi and Natalie Evans' book, *The Mixed-Race Experience*, they explain their use of the term, saying it is the term they feel comfortable with, what they're familiar with, while also acknowledging the complex histories and relationships of mixed-race people and terminology. 'The term "mixed" can also be dubious in that it can evoke negative connotations, such as being "confused", or "mixed up" or "unbalanced".'[2] What I love is the invitation they offer, that it is our choice how we define ourselves and that we can explore until we find what works.

I love the word mixed – mix it all together, cake recipes often say. Mix that batter, stir that pot, create a little chaos ...

*

Global north and global south

In 2021, I watched a panel on how to develop a culture of eating less meat where a tech bro discussed his fake meat company and explained how there is a long way to go as 'the developing world' was the biggest consumer of meat, pinpointing China as an example. I had an instant, physical reaction at the use of the phrase 'developing world'. I was flushed with anger and hurt. It was a sweeping statement of 'non-white' countries, with no context other than as 'a problem'. Not to mention that China has a centuries-old tradition of developing 'fake meat' due to Buddhism: in monasteries, imitation meats are an ancient tradition.

This incident made me think of how we talk about space, place and location. To talk about the ESEA experience and identity in the UK, we do need to talk about how these things interact and how we can define them. Within this book, and the discussion of race and identity as whole, it can be hard not to delve into binaries – them vs us, migrant vs native, white vs people of colour, West vs East. But, of course, things are not that simple. 'Global north' can feel interchangeable with 'Western', and 'global south' can seem like countries people used to call, and fake meat tech bros still call, 'developing countries'.

'Western' is something I relate to as a way of thinking, an outlook and a set of cultural norms or reference points. It is something that is not related to locale, but often a group of people within certain borders have a 'Western' understanding, or lexicon. The best way for me to describe how I navigate this term is when I am editing other writers. I ask: am I asking the writer for clarification because it sits outside of my Western understanding of this food or drink? If so, how do I ask for clarity but ensure that the explanation does not centre Western thinking or its sense of value?

I use the terms global north/south in relation to specific locations, but they are not about being in the north or south of the globe. The terms are instead an invitation to look at space in a whole new way, to understand these descriptions as power and interaction. The way I understand it is to think about how the south feeds the north – a historical dynamic that is still happening. With that in mind, you can find global south spaces within 'global north' countries and vice versa. At times, I do refer to the global south as a post-colonial place, but I try to approach it with an added layer of thinking about multiplicity within those borders and how stories reflect, relate to and/or interrogate the global north spaces in that locale.

Why 'developing' does not make sense within this discussion is because – what does 'developed' mean? Much Indigenous thinking is more developed than Western capitalist thinking, especially with the environment in mind. And, with the lack of access to heat and water, and the food apartheid that happens in 'global north' countries such as the UK, we could define many parts of Western European countries as 'developing'.

Us, we and 'ESEA'

I am but one note in a chain of voices, people and stories. This book is *a* beginning, not *the* beginning, a start within a contemporary conversation that has already been taken up in different formats and styles, such as the many books that have been published in the last few years – Angela Hui's *Takeaway*, Cecile Pin's *Wandering Souls*, Helena Lee's *East Side Voices*, Claire Kohda's *Woman, Eating*. I hope to sit among a growing canon of works by, for and exploring the ESEA experience in the UK.

Writing this book, I found that there has been little research on East and South East Asian immigration into the UK and the colonial world of those communities, but the work that has been done is impressive and in-depth. This book attempts to pull together those works and thinking, and try and paint a landscape of the British cultural environment within which we live. Therefore, I use the collective 'we', because I want solidarity and I want to be in solidarity. I use 'we' to refer to myself and others within the ESEA UK community. I believe in a collectiveness where we can be individuals that make change, and that in community we can honour and define difference. We can explore multiplicity in a way I hope will feel inclusive and generous and have a sense of togetherness: collectiveness and community in opposition to homogeneity. We are the group formally known, divided as, Chinese or Any Other Asian; we are Chinese *and* Many Other Asians. We are 'ESEA', an acronym that hopes to encompass and not divide. I use it as a way to be flexible and include, to not prioritise any one identity, but instead refer to a collection of identities of people with heritage from a region of the globe.

I do want to make the point that the use of 'us' and 'we' is not to make my voice a universal one, and isn't about me speaking for anyone, or being the voice of.

'Chinese' and 'Any Other Asian': what language does

The 2021 census recorded that of the 59.6 million residents in England and Wales, 83.2 per cent were born in the UK and 16.8 per cent, approximately 10 million people, were born outside of the UK.[3] 6.4 million of that number were born outside the EU.[4] 81.7 per cent of the usual residents in England and Wales identified as 'White'.[5] With this census, there were more options to self-identify than in previous years, and so there was an increase of people responding to the various 'Other' categories. How ethnicity is defined in the census is twofold. The first, high-level options are: 'Asian, Asian British or Asian Welsh'; 'Black, Black British, Black Welsh, Caribbean or African', 'Mixed or Multiple ethnic groups', 'White' or 'Other ethnic group'. Then there are nineteen available options at the second level.

Some of us would tick: 'Asian, Asian British or Asian Welsh'. Then, the next choices would be: 'Bangladeshi',

'Indian', 'Pakistani', 'Chinese' or 'Any other Asian background'. Between 2011 and 2021, there was barely an increase in those ticking 'Chinese', and only a small increase in 'Any other Asian background'. For me, first I choose 'Mixed or Multiple ethnic groups', which then gives me the options of: 'White and Asian'; 'White and Black African'; 'White and Black Caribbean' or 'Any other Mixed or Multiple background'. I choose 'Any other Mixed or Multiple background' because my understanding of 'Asian' in this context is Indian/Pakistani/Bangladeshi/Chinese; in 2021, the number of people selecting 'Asian, Asian British or Asian Welsh' had the largest increase since the 2011 census.[6]

As mentioned, there was the option to write in your specific ethnicity. This saw a further 287 ethnic groups being defined. Looking through this list I see – Chinese and White, Chinese and other Asian, Filipino, Indonesian, Japanese, Korean, Malaysian and more.[7] I also saw a lot of variations of whiteness – Norwegian, North American, German, Irish, etc. If I am honest, it chaffs me, as I think about how there isn't even an approximation of a representation of me in these forms – white and South East Asian (Indigenous at that!) – and still white people feel entitled to specifically define *how* they are white. It didn't even occur to me to write 'mixed Scottish New Zealander and Iban', I just put 'Other'. It feels engrained that I will not be represented within bureaucracy, that I seem to exist in a perpetual 'other'. But on the other hand, I do find it interesting that there seems to be a real need for nuanced identity, for all.

There are many options for 'White and X'; whiteness as central to all identities. Even when thinking of a mixed/ multiple identity, whiteness is where you start, and otherness is set against it. Where do you fit if you are Burmese and Indian? Sometimes I do choose 'Any Other Asian' on forms, without signalling my mixed-ness, because I am read as 'non-white' and I get frustrated that my whiteness within the concept of mixed-ness gets prioritised.

Information gained in the census allows for an understanding of what our society looks like and therefore informs policy and public funding. It allows for the government and local bodies to plan for the future in areas from healthcare and education, to transport and building homes. But if we are not properly represented, how will we be properly accounted for and recognised? How can planning be done if we can't even be seen? During Covid-19, it was reported that people of colour were more likely to die from the virus.[5] Understanding the granular would help us plan better for future health crises, at the very least.

I would argue that the brutal violence that happened to those of East and South East Asian heritage in reaction to Covid-19 is because of the official, bureaucratical language that gives a singular understanding of those that 'look like' they come from East Asia, particularly China. Every time someone is looking at a form that gives the option of 'Indian', 'Bangladeshi', 'Pakistani', 'Chinese' or 'Any other Asian', we are creating the idea that 'Chinese' is a sweeping identity and 'Other Asian' gathers up the rest from

East and South East Asia. This is restrictive. The scope for being Filipino, Malaysian, South Korean, Kurdish and more is unimaginable. And thus, 'Chinese' becomes a stand-in for all. To have 'Chinese' to be a blanket identity for all those with heritage from China also feels derivative. In my research and interviews, I have met people of ethnic Chinese heritage who chose to tick 'Other', as they didn't have a cultural identity with 'Chinese-ness'. And even those who are from the country of China don't see themselves as simply 'Chinese'.

Xiao Ma 马萧 was born in Gansu province, in northwest China. Her mother tongue is Chongxinhua, and she learnt Putonghua, or Mandarin, in school. She came to the UK in 2012 when she was in her early twenties for her master's degree. 'When I was in China, I would often be reminded by others that I am a Gansuren (Gansu person) when studying or travelling outside of Gansu,' Xiao tells me. She explains that these specifications on identity create place-based stereotypes and discrimination, and this is something she has lived with all her life. Coming to the UK, this definition of identity expanded to her being 'Chinese', leaving out any nuance of heritage – cultural and/or ethnic. When applying for an internship in London in 2013, the interviewer asked Xiao only one question, and it wasn't related to the job. 'I was surprised and asked, "Why didn't you ask me any questions about this internship?" They said: "I've worked with your people before, and I know your people work very hard." ' This exchange was shocking and Xiao had no idea how to respond. 'It sounded like a compliment, but it was not!'

Xiao found herself revisiting this conversation, particularly during the Covid-19 pandemic and the associated rise in anti-ESEA racism. 'I see myself as part of Chinese diasporas living in London, a city where I met the love of my life and a group of interesting souls whom I feel lucky to call friends, and where I grew into a critical heritage researcher and practitioner. London is my second home, but this is also the place where I became a *Chinese* person.'

By using 'Chinese' to define a group of people who are hugely diverse – ethnically, linguistically, culturally, socially – is to create homogeneity. Exploring this Anglophone context of the term 'Chinese' is part of what Xiao is currently researching (her PhD is looking at the cultural complexities of London's Chinatown and challenging a homogenising portrait of the area). 'In Chinese languages, as pointed out by many scholars including Gregory Lee, a wide range of terms are used by Chinese speakers in different contexts to reflect racial, ethnic, cultural and national nuances;* they are not always interchangeable! However, all these terms are usually translated as "Chinese" in English, which flattens and sometimes even misrepresents the nuances of people's identities and the complexities of their migration stories.'

---

* for example, Xiao explains to me: in Mandarin Chinese, they include Zhonghua minzu 中华民族, Huaren 华人, Tangren 唐人, Huaqiao 华侨, and Zhongguoren 中国人.

This flattening of identity, which happens when there is no space in bureaucracy for nuance, leads to violence. And this flattening spills over into everyday language. Cultural appropriation in art or food happens when value is not given to certain practices and people, and power or prestige is held for those already in power and/ or whiteness, and 'Asian' is considered at best a singular cuisine or at worst a marketing idea. The exoticism, laced with eroticism, in the way that East and South East Asian women are portrayed within media has created extreme vulnerability as language around identity creates otherness that dehumanises.

The language in law, policy-making and immigration makes legitimate the language of othering. Academic Nadine El-Enany explains in *Bordering Britain* that 'immigration is the tool that ensures that disposed peoples have no claim over what was stolen from them,' and that 'immigration law is also the prop used to teach white British citizens that what Britain plundered from its colonies is theirs and theirs alone'.[9] In this Western, global north, British space, it seems we don't really own anything, including our racial and ethnic identity. Defining people within this context of narrow racial lines and as 'not white' is the legacy of colonialism. It is also important to note that the definitions 'East Asian' and 'South East Asian' are terms created by colonial and imperial histories. Professor Gregory B. Lee, founding professor of China Studies at the University of St Andrews, writes that 'East Asia' was 'first popularised by the Japan's fascist, military regime between 1931 and 1945 when they invented the Greater East Asia Co-Prosperity Sphere or Dai Tōa Kyōeiken to mask, justify and advance their imperialist agenda'.[10] Lee goes on to explain that it was a term taken up by US agencies during the Cold War, dividing the world up into zones to be 'watched and studied', and 'thus, when the terms Oriental and Far Eastern were deemed to reek of the imperialist era, they were replaced by the more modern-sounding but equally politically problematic neo-colonialist designation of East Asia'. This has knock-on effects, Lee explains, such as university departments and academic centres defining studies by spaces carved up by a European and American 'vision of the world'.

But in contrast to these current narrowing definitions and a flattening of identity that has been built upon historical definitions, there has been a growing bonding and building of community, of East and South East Asian people connecting across the UK. Individuals have come together and taken back the narrative of what it means to have heritage from this region of the world. The term ESEA is a fairly new one.* Although it simplifies a group

---

* Sociologist Dr Diana Yeh writes: '"British East (and Southeast) Asian" has been in circulation "at least since the early 2000s"'.[11] But the acronym of ESEA – or at least including 'South East Asian' within the naming of these community groups – was not common until the pandemic, and the racism directed at many across the East and South East Asian identity spectrum is likely to have pushed this need to articulate a wider understanding of Asian identity.

of diverse people from vaguely the same part of the world, it doesn't flatten but rather brings together. The reason for this is because this term has sprung up from grass-roots organisations; from WhatsApp groups and Discord conversations, to real life nature walks and a (currently unofficial) 'ESEA Heritage Month'.

The organisation besea.n started during the pandemic as a group of ESEA women pooling resources, one of the founders, Mai-Anh Peterson, explained to me. This idea has now grown to be a volunteer-led advocacy platform that spotlights ESEA experiences. In 2021, besea.n organised an ESEA Heritage Month, which has run in September every year since. There is currently a Change.org petition calling for the official creation and recognition of the month. ESEA Sisters also began during the pandemic, as an online group that has become very much anchored in in-person events that are 'to share joy and resistance'. They create space for ESEA women, trans, non-binary and genderqueer folk to get together, including curated dinners, dance parties at Somerset House while you ice skate, natural walks and healing circles. At the start of the pandemic, actor Katie Leung invited me to a WhatsApp group for ESEA women in the arts; that group has now grown to include more than three hundred people. Although I am rather a silent participant, I can see that it is a vibrant space for discussion and support.

Finding a term to rally behind creates a language within which to thrive, a way to push for change and have a sense of belonging. The language around defining a broad group can bring people together, if it is from within the community rather than imposed. These new groups have of course developed because of previous community organising, particularly within the arts, such as BEAA (British East Asian Artists), which was launched in 2012, and BEATS (British East Asian in the Theatre and on Screen), which was launched in 2018.

On 1 September 2022, at an event to celebrate the launch of the paperback of *East Side Voices* at the Southbank Centre, British Indonesian poet Will Harris read the poem 'Strangers in a Hostile Landscape' by British Guyanese Chinese poet Meiling Jin, which was anthologised in *Watchers and Seekers: Creative Writing by Black Women in Britain*, published in the 1980s.[12] This poem tells a vivid, visual story that includes enslavement, indentured Chinese experiences in the Caribbean and feelings of displacement in the UK. It delves into empire and personifies the nations that are looking for 'unspeakable riches'. One idea of Blackness that was being developed at the time in Britain was that of a tool of solidarity to advocate for those who were being discriminated against because of their skin colour. This identity is often referred to as 'political Blackness', as it encompassed many ethnicities and racial heritages. The Southall Black Sisters were one of the key organisations doing this work of advocacy. Established in 1979, the Southall Black Sisters were – and still are – advocating for Black and minority women's rights. During this particular era of racial organising in the 1970s and 1980s, women of East Asian and South East Asian heritage were also part of these politically Black spaces. It is important to understand and acknowledge these acts of solidarity across identities and heritages, as well as the similarities and connectedness across communities. And indeed, an ethnically Chinese women who is from the Caribbean might not have felt 'East Asian', and might not – then or now – tick the 'Chinese' box on a census form.

One of the reasons I do like the term ESEA is because it forgoes the incorporation of 'British' in the definition of me. Not because I am not, or don't want to be, 'British', but to constantly couch my existence in my relationship to my nationality feels deferential – pleading to be accepted, to be recognised within bureaucracy and therefore having my legitimacy confirmed. Can I be all South East Asian *and* all British? Professor Lee writes, 'In the UK, Chinese immigrants and their descendants have long accepted being described as British Chinese, where Chinese is the noun and British the qualifying adjective. To use this term is to accept the primacy of ethnic identity over national identity.'[13] He sees this in opposition to the US, where you get to be Chinese/Japanese/Filipino American. 'Asian Americans did not wish to be seen as half American, they were all American.' 'American' is the noun. And so, 'the belongingness to Britain and the right to be called British becomes subsidiary to an "ethnic" or rather geopolitical name.' How we utilise these words to identify ourselves (or others choose how we should be identified) deeply affects our belonging. And if this space is our home, having a linguistic barrier to belonging makes us marginalised.

Among other things, Xiao is the curator of the 'East and Southeast Asians in the UK' Special Collection in the UK Web Archive. This serves as a tool to map and preserve the diverse websites created by individuals, groups and organisations who identify as 'ESEA' or identify their cultural or ancestral ties to a specific region in East Asia and/or South East Asia. It is a work-in-progress project, and Xiao is clear about the complications of using 'labels' and its imperfections, but this web archiving project helps see when ESEA groups started or 'rebranded' to being 'ESEA'. It is a 'time machine' of watching how language develops.

My worry with language and terms of identification is that they will get co-opted. I fear that the collectiveness of ESEA can easily be turned into a superficial sticking plaster. When the political nature is left out, solidarity loses its power and effectiveness. The Golden Chopsticks Awards, an awards ceremony within the UK catering industry, now claims that it recognises East and South East Asian cuisine in the UK, and yet to my mind there is insufficient interrogation into what is meant by that, or what that entails. The awards have often been awarded to East Asian establishments and Ivy Asia was a finalist in

2022. Ivy Asia comes across as a rich white man's exotic fantasy of an entire continent – Orientalism dialled up to bust* (more details in Chapter 6 on Food). I think it would be more fun and interesting if the awards just said it was celebrating cuisines that used chopsticks! The nuance that could be explored would be amazing. ESEA as a collective identity to belong to should stay at a grassroots level so that it can work as a point of solidarity, activism and advocacy. As it moves beyond that, then we need be specific and nuanced in our language. When bureaucracy and systems come into play, we need to be careful to not fall back into tick boxes. I don't want to open the census form in 2031 and find a box for 'East and South East Asian', or worse, simply 'ESEA' – to be reduced to an acronym.

We use the term ESEA now, and for now. There is so much incredible work and truly 'for the first time' moments of collective solidarity and community activism. But we are part of a solidarity movement/s that started long before us, and will continue to shift and change and find new language long after us. I feel so indebted to those people before me, such as those that identified as politically Black, so that I can have this language of difference, and the language of solidarity, and explore those gritty dynamics of power. And again, it is a reminder of using language to not silo or flatten but to engage with power and to collaborate. Academic Diana Yeh writes that 'the

---

* imho

mobilisation of "British East and Southeast Asian" as a form of identity-based politics can be an expansive force that opens up, rather than forestalls, solidarities across racial, gendered, sexual and ableist and other forms of oppression'.[14] We are intrinsically connected to all marginalised communities, and those with violent colonial histories.

'You have a durian tattoo, right?' is the first thing that Sarah Owen says to me on the phone. Sarah's mother is of Chinese Malaysian heritage, and Sarah is the Labour MP for Luton North. She is the first Labour MP of ESEA background and the second ESEA MP for the UK. 'I hate durian but I have this vivid memory of my mother chasing us round with her durian breath.' Oh how this tricksy fruit, the durian, seeps into so many of our lives!

The durian has become my talisman, my calling card, my love and – at times – my whole identity. It was deep love at first bite. When I was a child, I would eat so much durian I would make myself sick. I am sorry to my mother who had to apologise profusely to a horrified businessman in a Singapore airport whose briefcase I vomited all over after a durian feast before flying.

The durian is something that takes up all your senses. It is heavy, covered in spikes, with a pungent aroma that creeps into every single place imaginable for miles around it (if not literal miles, it sure feels like it). Some will say the scent is unpleasant, but for me it is the promise of joy. Its taste is sweet and savoury, almost like sautéed onions, and it will take up your whole palate. The flesh differs between fruits, and can be soft or firm – but even the texture fills your mouth. The durian encompasses you.

Often when I arrived in Kuching, my dad would have sourced a durian and we would gather to eat it all together. Aunty Mary would open it with an enormous knife and we'd sit outside, weighing up if we thought it was good or not. It was best if we had a few durians of different varieties to compare.

But the story of durian, and the language that gets used around durian in the West, is one of barely concealed racism. A British chocolatier, Paul A. Young, used the durian flavour as a representation of abused women in 2019. One in four women in the UK have been victims of domestic violence and, as part of a campaign undertaken in collaboration with non-profit organisation, Women's Trust, to highlight domestic abuse in Britain, Young's chocolate brand showed one durian-flavoured chocolate in a box alongside three strawberry-flavoured chocolates. The durian chocolate was named 'chocolat dégoûtant' ('disgusting chocolate'), and described as having a 'vomit-like taste'.[15] It is hugely problematic that this equated victims of domestic abuse to a fruit he and others find disgusting. But it is also an issue to be degrading foods beloved of various people who live in the UK. He apologised, explaining it was not an intention to be disrespectful to someone's culture.* But I have seen many white people describe durian in articles, on social media, and in casual conversation with language of disgust. 'To call a fruit difficult because it is unfamiliar to me and I do not like it would be ridiculous. A failure of imagination,' writes Kate Lebo in the durian chapter of her 2021 book, *The Book of Difficult Fruit*.[16] Young and so many have failed in their imagination.

I tell the story of the durian because it is easy to see how language used thoughtlessly can risk projecting racism, and through this rather obvious, and pungent, example we can see that it is not only with durian, or strong-smelling ingredients, that this happens. Derogatory language around non-Western food is seen often, and it is incredibly hurtful and dehumanises. Food is one of those threads that stays with you, even across multiple generations, as a way to reach back to a home you once knew, or know through the stories from the generations before you. To hear the words of disgust about tastes that give you a sense of identity can strip you of a sense of home and can make your identity feel less than; that you yourself are disgusting. We are told we are what we eat, and so these reactions feel personal. Do we give up our

---

* Paul Young's apology said: 'I'm truly sorry that the messaging on this partnership has distracted from the true intention – to raise awareness for the shocking statistics around domestic abuse. When I was first approached to work on this campaign, it was never our intention to bring negative attention or be disrespectful to anyone's culture, and I am wholeheartedly sorry that it has had this effect.'[17]

foods to make ourselves, and the spaces we cook, eat, live in, more palatable for others?

In her 2005 book, *For Space*, geographer Doreen Massey wrote, 'arriving in a new place means joining up with, somehow linking into, the collections of interwoven stories of what that place is made of'.[18] It is with this as inspiration that I want to talk about the language of being a migrant, of being racialised and of being from multiple homes – for loving durian *and* scones with jam.

When we are from 'somewhere else', or of diaspora, there is often a feeling of being caught between two worlds, between two cultures. But this language breaks us down to halves, to being not fully drawn. As well as finding a way to exist in a world that others us, it is also important to find the language to belong, for ourselves. Often when we speak of migration, we can picture a thread that pulls us back to a centre, to 'home', to memory, to childhood, to a nostalgia. But the UK is (also) our home and this may not be our final stop; our children may move on, they may find love and safety in places far and wide. How will they negotiate the concept of migration? We can't just stop in the now. We should be able to imagine a future for us, beyond the *now*. I refuse to be caught between. I want to be multiple. There is joy in being one of many threads of stories that make a place.

When researching my PhD, I came across the idea of 'dynamic flow'. This concept was coined by Soda Ryoji, a Japanese anthropologist who researched Iban culture. It is based on the idea of expanding space, as opposed to migration as a linear experience. The place of 'home' expands with you as you travel, allowing you to be figuratively in multiple spaces of home at once.

> Like my Iban forebears, I am a migrant who adapts to the environment; building, planting, nurturing and then moving on to begin again. Like my Iban cousins I am a migrant who calls more than one place home. My story becomes interwoven with each location, and each location becomes a part of my identity. I also bring the past into new locations. Memories and identities that were created and developed in previous situations get utilised in different ways and/or get expressed in new ways. These are intersections of my identity that are articulated for each new space, and I have a choice in how they get presented.[19]

I wrote in my essay for the 2022 anthology *East Side Voices*.

We are building daily home through very simple actions, such as cooking or cleaning, small rituals that tie us to a place and slowly build home. So we get to be of both or multiple places, or all identities – British *and . . .*

This is difficult, of course, because we are navigating a space where language has been used to make us not feel welcome. But I want to build new language, even if just for ourselves, that lets us not be caught, suspended between two worlds. 'There are no strict rules and procedures governing the performance of Iban ritual activities.

Iban may and do, through dreams and personal experience, either alter the well-established rites or simply ignore [them],' my dad wrote in his PhD.[20] It is this practical sense of innovation, while still holding a reverence for ceremony, that is built into my sense of identity. Let us dream and be practical, let us rely on experience and choose how we want to ritualise and ceremonialise our lives, let us ignore stories that damage. Let us be messy, be mixed, be multiple and be anchored in the now and in the past, and to our future. We have so many new stories to be telling and language to develop to express our existence.

Durian is now a part of my London life. It can't be a garden party – especially a Gawai* – without a durian. I open it, half drunk on white wine, on my knees in the garden. And just to get one is an adventure; traipsing it home across London on public transport, from the Vietnamese shop in Hackney; no matter how many layers of newspaper and plastic bags it is in, a lingering scent escapes. Durian is my language of home. I want to know and hear what others' are.

* Gawai is the harvest festival celebration of the Indigenous (Dayak) people of Sarawak, of which the Iban are part of.

Chapter 2

Empire and Migration

It is −1 degrees outside and the dog is refusing to get out of bed. I don't blame him. I've yet to put the heating on, trying to push back the need for as long as possible, and the bedroom is cold. The UK has eased out of pandemic fear and plunged headfirst into a cost-of-living crisis. The world feels precarious; the structures we live in don't feel fit for purpose.

When I turn the heating on and open the curtains, I see that the snow has arrived and a magical landscape straight out of books from my childhood appears before me. The world of Streatfeild's *Ballet Shoes*, of Dickens novels, of all the Christmas-related imagery I grew up with – while I ate strawberries on the beach on 25 December – is laid out, in my own garden. I left home for the promise of this. White winters and cosy pubs. No one told me of food banks, underinvested transport services, rough sleepers, price-gouging energy companies, all of which combined with a cold snap and beautiful snow make for a dangerous landscape. The dream of empire melts fast when faced with reality.

That's what empire is and was – a dream. It was a dream that we felt keenly in our (post) colonial spaces, where we heard stories of streets paved with gold along with white Christmases. It was, and still is, a dream for those in the UK too. This collective nostalgia for, and of, an empire is at the heart of recent historical moments. Understanding our colonial history is also a way into exploring how Britain sees itself and sees the world.

In June 2016, days before the Brexit vote, Irish writer and broadcaster Peter Geoghegan wrote for Al Jazeera: 'The desire to regain Britain's colonial prowess has provided the subtext for much of the referendum debate. "Let's make Britain great again," declared former London mayor Boris Johnson and other prominent leave advocates [. . .] And when was Britain greatest? When it ruled half the world, of course.'[1] The brutal realities of that 'ruling' are forever hidden, Geoghegan wrote.*

We saw this reflection of empire when the Queen died in 2022, as an outpouring of grief hid realities; as *Guardian* columnist Afua Hirsch wrote days afterwards: 'During her reign, the BBC tells us, colonies "gained independence", but there's no mention of those who were imprisoned, shot and killed in the struggles – from the Gold Coast to Cyprus, India and Malaya – that were required to win it.'[2]

* Routledge's *Journal of Postcolonial Writing* published a special issue titled 'Writing Brexit: Colonial Remains' and described the departure as narcissistic: 'It identifies and historicizes Britain's departure from the EU as the result of a long-standing process, rooted in persisting imperial attitudes and, arguably, narcissistic yearnings.'[3]

The British Empire began because of a desire for goods. In pursuit of financial gain, European colonialism created the capitalist system in which we now live. The story of empire is one of power and might. Yet in its nostalgic retelling, it completely erases the people within the borders of colonial spaces, placing Britain at the centre. As historian and author Alex von Tunzelmann writes: 'In the beginning, there were two nations. One was a vast, mighty and magnificent empire, brilliantly organised and culturally unified, which dominated a massive swathe of earth. The other was an underdeveloped, semi-feudal realm, riven by religious factionalism and barely able to feed its illiterate, diseased and stinking masses. The first nation was India. The second was England.'4

Although about South Asia, and not the regions this book delves into, this quote helps reframe our understanding of the British Empire. European colonialism needed to dominate spaces to extract goods and labour. Britain's desire for labour led to the transatlantic slave trade and indentured servitude, as well as eradicating native populations and knowledge. To attempt to justify these actions, the European empires constructed systems of othering, so creating the idea of whiteness. At best, agents of empire infantilised those they saw as 'subjects', introducing the idea of the noble savage who could be guided to a Christian God. At worst, these agents enacted terrible violence upon people, communities and culture. In imperial propaganda and rhetoric, colonised spaces and people were framed as uncivilised and in need of saving;

a far cry from the reality of complex communities and well-established global connections.

The colonial framing of the global south as spaces of historic emptiness, or disorder, or with naïve peoples, lingers through language, policy, the arts, food and the reaction to a pandemic. It continues to cause violence in devastating ways.

The story of colonialism for me begins before the idea of a British Empire was conceived. We all have our ways into a story. My understanding of colonialism and its beginnings is through the Mongol Empire, specifically a favourite book of mine, *Invisible Cities* by Italo Calvino. It's a fictional story of explorer and trader Marco Polo telling Emperor Kublai Khan about a myriad of cities, a detailed and poetical description of place. It is really a telling and retelling of Marco Polo's home, Venice. It captured my imagination because it told of how we can conceive of place and home; and the idea of homesickness, nostalgia and being a migrant. But what this book made me realise is the centuries-old relationship that exists between Europe and Asia.

Mongolia is part of the East and South East Asian region, and the ancient Mongol Empire was the biggest in history;* therefore it seems appropriate that this is the beginning of the British Empire, for me. Merchants brought

---

* It is worth noting that the Mongol Empire was also brutal and violent; like all empires it expanded through violence and war.

spices to England because the trade route overland was stabilised by the Mongolian reign, so that goods from India, China, the Indonesian archipelago and beyond were able to traverse across what came to be known as the Silk Road(s). Before European empires, there was a vibrant trade route throughout Asia, with Europe at the tail-end. England benefitted from a sophisticated and flourishing trade system before it became the aggressor. The Company of Grocers, established by the late 1300s, was the English guild responsible for the importation of spices and various colonial goods. It has a camel atop its coat of arms to express how important the animal was in bringing trade across land to England.

'Medieval European food, or at least that enjoyed by the more economically comfortable classes, was perfumed with a great variety of spices,' Paul Freedman writes in his book *Out of the East: Spices and the Medieval Imagination*.[5] The promise of profit turned this enjoyment into big business. Europeans realised that if the middlemen – Muslim merchants, who were already a problematic figure in the Christian European psyche – could be cut out, then great gains could be had. With the fall of Constantinople in 1453, and the banning of Christian merchants, there came an even more urgent need to get direct access to these goods. In 1492, Christopher Columbus, an Italian under Spanish commission, sailed west from Europe in hope of finding access to the Spice Islands (now known as the Banda Islands in Indonesia). He wasn't successful, and instead landed on what is now known as the Bahamas.* It was the Portuguese nobleman Vasco da Gama that made that first sea trip across to Asia. He set sail east, navigating around the Cape of Good Hope, and arrived in what is now Kerala in 1498. Both these journeys brought untold wealth to the Spanish and Portuguese monarchies and began the European colonial project in earnest.

1543 saw Spain laying claim to what we now know as the Philippines, led by Ruy López de Villalobos who sailed from Mexico. The South and South East Asian regions were becoming tangible places to Europeans; the unknown was becoming ownable. England was desperate to be there. In 1600, Queen Elizabeth I gave charter to a stock-joint organisation of merchants, the 'Governor and Company of Merchants of London Trading into the East-Indies', commonly known as the English East India Company (EIC), to oust the embedded Spanish and Portuguese. This charter was to last fifteen years, giving the company a monopoly to operate in the Indian Ocean under the crown's purview. King James I then extended the charter, and monopoly, indefinitely with only one criteria: the company had to turn a profit. To quote von Tunzelmann again, 'Thus a beast was created whose only objective was money... pure capitalism unleashed for the first time in history.' She further explains: 'it was a private

---

* Although Columbus never went to the largest North American landmass, this was the beginning of European colonialism in the Americas; Columbus's legacy is one of great violence.

empire of money, unburdened by conscience, rampaging across Asia, unfettered into the 1850s.'[6]

Britain's relationship with East and South East Asia began because of and through the EIC. The Straits Settlements, which were a collection of ports from the island of Penang off the coast of the Malaysian peninsula to Singapore, were created in the mid-1820s after drawing lines in the waters and lands with the Dutch. These ports were ruled by the EIC out of India. On advice in 1819 from Stamford Raffles, an EIC official based in Sumatra, 'securing' Singapore was a crucial need for trade between India and China. The Temenggong of Johor,* who had sovereignty over Singapore, ceded the island to the British in 1819.[7]

During this time, China was a fairly self-sufficient region and didn't want any of the goods that the EIC had to trade, and the EIC didn't want to spend silver (which they had a shortage of) to purchase the goods they wanted from China. Opium was legal in England, but it was prohibited in China, and so the EIC found a way to illegally trade opium, grown in colonised India, with China in exchange for tea. In 1893, the Viceroy of Hunan and Jiangxi, Lin Zexu, established an anti-opium campaign, burning the equivalent of two million pounds' (in today's currency) worth of British opium in public.

---

* A senior councilman/administrative position appointed by the Sultan of Johor, at this time it would have been Ungku Abdul Rahman.

This resulted in the Anglo-Chinese War, known commonly as the First Opium War, from 1839–42. Britain and China signed a treaty granting Britain rule over Hong Kong island, although neither party were happy with the agreement; China was made to pay for the burnt opium, and the English were unhappy that opium was still illegal and saw Hong Kong as a barren island with a scattering of houses. But it proved to be a very strategic spot in the next Anglo-Chinese War and it was designated a 'free port', a place where people could easily trade without tariffs or customs. The treaty did not mention opium and so the British continued importing it, still very much as an illicit product.

Britain acquired Kowloon and Stonecutters Island after the second Anglo-Chinese War (1856–60) for an annual rent of 500 silver dollars. In 1898 New Territories, a region of Hong Kong stretching up to the border with mainland China, was also leased to Britain. The handover of Hong Kong and the New Territories back to China happened in 1997. The space of Hong Kong was structured as other colonial spaces, with the British forming the establishment. 'This was a product of self-confidence and racial arrogance that came with the power of empire,' historian Steven Tsang writes.[8]

The end of the EIC's rule came in 1858, when lands and regions were 'handed over' to the British Empire, under the reign of Queen Victoria I. Under British rule, colonialism expanded, particularly in South East Asia, with the underlying function of financial gain for the crown and country. The EIC's dominance, and the further British expansion, was instrumental in the movement of hundreds of thousands of people and a complete reshaping of the world.

Where are you from?

This question alludes to 'why are you here?', questioning the legitimacy of your existence in a space. The answer is colonialism, 'because you were there',* but that is rarely understood, especially by the person asking. In his 2021 book, *We're Here Because You Were There: Immigration and the End of Empire,* Ian Sanjay Patel writes, 'Only by retelling the story of immigration, not as a domestic national story confided to the British Isles but as a diverse international story connected to empire, can we begin to see it clearly.'[9] His book outlines how empire and immigration are related to current understandings of race and belonging in the UK. It is therefore important to understand how we – ESEA communities – came to be in the UK and how that link with a colonial past is crucial to understanding why we are here, and why we chose to be here.

The 1800s saw the biggest movement of people in world history. The abolition of slavery in the first part of the century gave way to a system for indentured workers

---

* British Sri Lankan writer Ambalavaner Sivanandan's words, in response to anti-immigrant British society in post-war Britain.

47

and other exploited labour, and a continued migration of racialised peoples for work. Academic and sugar expert Sidney W. Mintz wrote that to solve the 'problem' of labour, after the abolishment of slavery, the British looked to agrarian cultures elsewhere in the empire: 'It was thanks to their [indentured workers and other colonial subjects'] brawn and suffering that the transition from enslaved to proletarian labour would be realised.'[10]

An indentured worker is contracted to work, unpaid, for a set amount of time; although technically voluntarily entering this contract, people were seen as belonging to their employers. The British Empire looked to its colonies to supply a workforce in plantations globally – from sugarcane fields in the West Indies and the Indian Ocean islands, to rubber and tea plantations and rice fields in South East and South Asia. This included Javanese, Chinese, Japanese, Pacific Islanders and Indians – as the sun traversed the globe, so did the people of the Victorian British Empire, the sun never setting on the backs of these workers. According to Patel, an estimated '50 million Europeans, 50 million Chinese and 30 million Indians migrated globally' during the nineteenth century.[11] The largest group of labourers were the Chinese, and they didn't just come from colonial spaces, such as Hong Kong or South East Asia.

A large number of Chinese migrants moved to the British West Indies and, although they were indentured, there was a sense of agency that might not have been available to other groups. Between 1859 and 1866, there were agencies in Hong Kong and Canton, run by Chinese people to facilitate the migration; in particular, the Suriname Immigration Company, a private company that brought seven ships from Hong Kong to the West Indies between 1865 and 1869.[12] There was an agreement that plantation owners and the local colonial government would pay and facilitate these Chinese (mostly men) to return home after five years. But many plantation owners reneged on this agreement, resulting in a termination of the China-based organised migration of these workers.

After the five years, Chinese workers often chose to stay in the West Indies. And later a further contingent of Chinese migrants came to the region (and travelled further afield to Latin American) due to a lack of economic and social stability in China after the end of the imperial power in the early twentieth century.[13] In the late 1800s, Chinese communities had mostly left the farming life in the West Indies and moved into urban areas and townships, taking up roles as traders. Operating within a class and colour hierarchy of the colonial and plantation structure of society, they were able to act as middlemen. During the Windrush generation, and subsequent generations, many Caribbean Chinese people came to the UK through that Commonwealth connection.

The late 1800s and early twentieth century saw a small group of seamen migrate from Hong Kong to the UK, in particular via shipping trade routes. This British-governed region was already seen as a place for European shipping companies to hire sailors, and Southern Chinese men had been travelling across the globe for some time via European ships. Most sailors returned home after working abroad on ships, but a few 'jumped ship' and made homes in European cities.

The Alfred Holt & Company shipping group, based in Liverpool and founded in 1866, was one of the main English employers of Chinese sailors. Liverpool's Chinese community is one of the oldest in Europe due to this seafaring tradition, which peaked in the 1920s and 1930s, and was phased out after the Second World War. It is important to note that these men were often exploited and were paid far less than their European counterparts.

The history of Chinese sailors in the UK is a dark tale that has only recently been acknowledged. During the Second World War, approximately 20,000 Chinese seamen were part of the shipping industry based out of Liverpool and became integral to the war effort, responsible for supply lines, fuelling and refuelling the Navy. These men built lives and families in Britain. Yet many of them were deported after the war, despite the country's dire need of labour to rebuild it. This deportation was decided on 19 October 1945 in a meeting attended by thirteen men, including a senior Home Office official, representatives of the Foreign Office, Liverpool police and the Ministry of War Transport. This decision was to be kept out of the public domain and remain secret.

These men were rounded up without the opportunity to say goodbye to their families, and most of their wives and children had no idea what had happened. It was only the declassification of these files in the 1990s that allowed the descendants of these men to investigate. In 2021, questions were raised in Parliament by Liverpool Riverside MP Kim Johnson on behalf of her constituents, and a *Guardian* investigation was published,[14] leading to the launch of an internal government investigation.

A number of the Chinese men who came to the UK from the late nineteenth century set up food businesses or laundries. Laundries were appealing as they needed little start-up capital and were not public-facing, and so knowing English (well) wasn't a priority. A report ('The Chinese in Britain' by A. Shang in 1984) states that in 1931, 800 Chinese laundries existed in Britain.[15] Before the Second World War, the Chinese food establishments in the UK were casual, cheap noodle shops for other Chinese customers, but the 1950s saw a 'restaurant boom'; between 1957–1964, the number of Chinese restaurants doubled. This period saw a very different Chinese establishment appear, and 'in 1965, five Chinese restaurants opened in rapid succession in an obscure street in London's West End,' James L. Watson writes.[16] Chinese establishments began to cater for white British customers, and thus Gerard Street and London's new Chinatown was born (originally a Chinatown was situated in Limehouse, East London near the docks). Watson, an anthropologist specialising in Chinese emigrants to London, has a rather scathing tone when describing the British public, whom he says 'did not "discover" Chinese food until post World War

II'. In Watson's writing, there is an acknowledgement that this community and their food had been in the country for a while.

Because Hong Kong and the New Territories were considered part of the British Empire, there were various types of British passports issued to those born in the region during the period of colonialism, from the mid-nineteenth century onwards. This meant that, although full citizenship or access to rights weren't granted, there was a route to migrate to the UK from the area. From the 1950s onwards, there continued to be a strong connection between Chinese migrants and the hospitality industry, fuelled by immigration policy that allowed those from the British-governed regions to come to the UK and work in certain industries and jobs. In some instances, earlier migrants who had begun expanding their businesses paid the passage for (mostly) men to come and work in their restaurants. As a result, Chinese takeaways and restaurants across the UK have been responsible for a sea change in the food of Britain.

The years after the Second World War saw many shifts in immigration policy, relating to the declarations of independence from many colonies and Britain's changed relationships with empire. To confirm the idea of imperialism and strengthen the then-new concept of the 'Commonwealth', the British Nationality Act of 1948 was introduced the year after Indian independence. In practice, this meant that in the late 1940s and 1950s, many people from non-white Commonwealth spaces moved to the UK; that number was approximately 500,000[17] and included the 492 people on the HMT *Empire Windrush* (1948). People came from the colonies to rebuild Britain post-war, but alongside this drive, the government decided to encourage and give citizenship to European nationals, in particular Eastern Europeans.* There were concerns that British [white] 'stock' needed to be 'replenished'[18] after the war, coupled with a desire to reinforce the notions of whiteness. Britain was welcoming former and current colonial subjects to a hostile space, with the empire defined and redefined on an almost yearly basis as states continued to gain independence – Malaysia in 1957, and North Borneo, Sarawak and Singapore in 1963.

The Commonwealth Immigrants Act came into effect in 1962, which meant only those with a work permit from the Commonwealth were allowed into the UK. This was the first of a number of changes to immigration law that formally racialised UK immigration. Academic Nadine El-Enany refers to this shift in policy as colonial violence, and notes that when the bill was being discussed in 1961, it was the first time that people of 'United Kingdom and Colonies' were being distinguished as either immigrants or British subjects.[19] Previously 'subjects' had referred to all those who were part of the British Empire, but now

---

* Ian Sanjay Patel notes that in 1947 this included 130,000 former members of the Polish armed forces, and British nationality was extended to them.

those from colonial or post-British colonial states were to be referred to as 'immigrants', a label that had been previously used only for those outside of the British Empire. The 'subjects' were now people born in, or had passports issued by the governments of, Britain and Ireland, who were predominantly white. The 1971 Immigration Act included an addition to the policy, defining that those who were born or whose parent was born in the UK would have the right to abode, meaning they could live and work without restrictions.

The concept of British citizenship as we know it today did not come into existence until 1981. Before that, you were a citizen of the United Kingdom and Colonies – this emphasised the breadth of empire, but often restricted racialised people within this empire. The 1981 British Nationality Act was when Britain, for the first time, defined itself entirely as a space set within hard borders. The British identity became the specific location of the united kingdoms – England, Wales, Scotland and Northern Ireland. Immigration and Britain's relationship with its ex-colonies continued to change and is still in constant transformation. The terms of working-holiday visas with white settler colonies were constantly in flux when I was in my twenties, and no doubt various visas will continue to be, as relationships between nations shift and change.

In 2020 China introduced the National Security Law (NSL) to Hong Kong in response to protests that had taken place the year before.* This law made various dissenting acts illegal. In 2021 forty-seven protesters, pro-democracy campaigners and activists were arrested in one of the biggest crackdowns under this law; they were accused of 'overthrowing' the government and officially charged with 'conspiracy to commit subversion under national security law'. As of May 2024, thirty-one of the defendants had pleaded guilty, fourteen were found guilty, and two had been acquitted. Global criticism of the trials was swift, such as Human Rights Watch's acting China director, Maya Wang, saying the convictions were against 'democratic political process and the rule of law'.[20]

In response to the NSL, in January 2021 those in Hong Kong with British National (Overseas) identities were able to apply for a visa to move to the UK.† The home secretary at the time, Priti Patel, said: 'This status recognised the special and enduring ties the UK has with those people as a result of our role in Hong Kong before

---

* It is worth noting that these weren't the first pro-democracy protests in Hong Kong; one of the most recent and well-known was known as the Umbrella Movement, in 2014. This was in response to proposed elections, but only with candidates approved by China. Umbrellas were used by protesters to protect themselves from tear gas, and most of the protesters were students.

† Those in Hong Kong and the New Territories were able to register as British National (Overseas) before 1 July 1997. This meant you had a British passport, but it did not give you the right to work or live in the UK – although there were some visas and citizen routes, if you met certain criteria.

1997. Now that China, through its actions, has changed the circumstances that BN(O) citizens find themselves in, it is right that we should change the entitlements which are attached to BN(O) status.' This was offered because the Conservative government stated China was in breach of the 1984 Sino-British Joint Declaration,* which stated 'one country, two systems'.† Patel further noted her 'generosity' of offering this immigration route.[21]

When looking at the history of immigration policy and law in Britain, I see a nation that is not able to look at its past through clear eyes. During colonialism, there was a sense of freer movement, but often enforced movement for labour, and rhetoric that appeared inclusive, albeit brutal and violent in its framing. Nevertheless, these masses of lands, although distant from each other, were part of a 'oneness' of the British Empire. Yet throughout the process of decolonisation, there was a desperate desire to define Britain's identity as white, and to control who got to access that space of whiteness. And in tandem there

---

* From the Gov.uk official page on the immigration route: 'The UK Government's decision to introduce a new Hong Kong BN(O) Visa follows the imposition by the Chinese Government of a national security law on Hong Kong that restricts the rights and freedoms of the people of Hong Kong and constitutes a clear and serious breach of the Sino-British Joint Declaration.' [22]

† 'One country, two systems' refers to an agreement that came into effect in 1997 when Hong Kong was 'returned' to China. This is part of Hong Kong's constitution (the Basic Law) and sets out a structure of governance for the territory, including freedom of assembly and freedom of speech.

was a need to uphold a sense of 'greatness' as proof that the violent assertion over its colonies was indeed 'good'.

It is important to remember that behind these policies are people, stories, families. Immigration response and policy shapes British life. For example, Thatcher's government's response to Vietnamese refugees fleeing conflict dehumanised a community. In 1979, Britain agreed to participate in the United Nations High Commissioner for Refugees' scheme to support those refugees, but with great reluctance. A key point to the plan was to disperse new arrivals throughout the country, without a thought of community, which created deep isolation for many. The political language at the time framed vulnerable people as 'burdens' on British society, and not people seeking safety. 'Dispersal, then, would simultaneously reduce costs for, and demand on, statutory services and voluntary support in any one area, while diluting the presence of the refugees to the point of near-invisibility,' writes Becky Taylor in the article 'Our Most Foreign Refugees: Refugees from Vietnam in Britain', as part of the *Palgrave Studies in Migration History* series.[23] Acceptable immigration was one that made the people disappear. This narrative and approach would have a lasting impression on anyone. And we see this rhetoric today.

These immigration policies were not always about one-way migration and were anchored in an idea of labour. My friend Vera Chok, an actor, writer and artist of Malaysian Chinese origin, explains that her parents were at teacher training college in the UK in the late

1950s and early 1960s, with the objective of going back to Malaysia to then teach English. 'My dad says that the scheme was started by the British, probably to thank the Malayans and funded by the profits of the [colonial Malaysian] rubber and tin industry,' she says. 'By 1969, my dad was in Leeds University doing an MA in English Literature. It was likely he was on a scholarship because he came from a very poor family but was very bright.' Another friend, food writer Jenny Lau, explains to me that her parents were in the UK, working for the NHS in the early 1970s, in London. Her mother, a Chinese Malaysian from Sarawak, came over at eighteen and her father, a Cantonese doctor from Hong Kong, came to the UK after studying in Germany.

Liew Chee Cheng, who is also known as Linda, told me about working in the NHS in the 1970s. 'There were a lot of Malaysians training to be nurses then, and we'd come home and share our chicken curry,' Linda said. Those moments were important, because it was a real culture shock to be in London. 'You know, we thought London was paved in gold, but when I came – looking at the buildings, the weather, it was such a letdown. We were quite lucky in London, we had the docks and the Malaysian ships would dock there and we would be invited to the parties and get the food as well. We'd do a late shift, then have an overnight party and get home at six o'clock in the morning.' And once they were all working as nurses, the community feeling expanded. Linda's daughter Suyin talks about an old group photo from that time: 'When the nurses would go out with their children, they would call themselves the United Nations, because they were from the Philippines, Jamaica, Malaysia, all these different countries and all these kids. That was quite a cool moment in time.'

The story of empire and migration is also an idea of what is home, what our relationship is to Britain. Diaspora is a word that means to disperse from an origin, a homeland – every time I say it, I picture the scattering of a dandelion. Blowing on the fluffy white head, making a wish and watching the aerodynamic seeds catch a breeze. It is a romantic idea, and this image is against a blue sky and in soft, warm sun. It is a vision of new beginnings, adventure and the concept of finding a place to settle to spread roots and grow. But, of course, we know that migrants, and those who are finding new homes, don't always land gently to take up a rooted and secure identity. We, those of diasporic heritage, talk of being 'diaspora' and 'migrants'. This idea of travel and movement and journey is related to our identity, *even* if we can trace a history in this country for generations. Even if there is a box we *can* tick on a census form.

This idea of scattering, of dispersing from a central origin of home is also one that is beginning to feel more and more at odds with how I see my – and others' – identity. Because this land, this Britain, is ours too. This *is* our homeland, our 'motherland'; our sense of rootedness in it is based on narratives that we grew up learning. I say this as someone who arrived here, but those who have generations of history here must feel this even more keenly. How can we be diasporic when our entire educational and cultural upbringing is rooted in the greatness of Britain? While in the sunshine, we dreamt of a white Christmas.

The colonial project was one that hyped up Britain. It developed this idea of the 'British subject' to strengthen the concept of empire, enfolding a native population into an identity of a place that was so distant. It was a way to have control, to ensure that the people they were ruling over didn't see themselves as independent. English became the national language, legal systems were based on British law, and books told stories of a country of fields and lashings of ginger beer. I am here because the landscape of Arthur Ransome's *Swallows and Amazons* was more familiar to me than my childhood one of rivers and jungles. My teenage knowledge of King Henry VIII's wives blinded me to learning about Māori history, the history of the land I was growing up on. Deep in my bones, I felt like I was meant to be in the UK, and that my arrival would give me a place to finally belong.

But we arrive and we are described as migrant and diasporic, an identity of non-belonging. I grew up mostly in a settler state, long after the collapse of the British Empire, and I am still imprinted with Britain as an identity for which I am a part of and should aspire to. This is home because it was sold to me as such, and it is home because the colonies built it. El-Enany writes, in the very first paragraph of her book *Bordering Britain*, that 'Britain's modern state infrastructure, including its welfare state, was dependent on resources required through colonial conquest.'[24] The NHS that celebrated its seventy-five-year anniversary in 2023 was built on, and still exists on, employees from the (ex) colonies – a detail that is missing from many mainstream conversations. The wealth gained from resources extracted from the colonies built the foundations of modern Britain. The infantilisation of colonial 'subjects' means that we are framed as children apart from their mother. There are so many ties to anchor us and draw us to this country.

How do we, *can* we, reframe this? Jenny Lau says that she has come to realise that 'diaspora' is less relevant to her as a label and she has started recently to use 'transnational'. Jenny says, ' "Transnational" accounts for the fact that I was born in the UK, grew up in Hong Kong and from the age of eleven moved to London but always with one base (and one half of my nuclear family) in my childhood city. It's also slightly different to what third culture kids experience in terms of identity formation and notions of home. These distinctions are important to make. I feel that I can empathise with diasporic individuals but do not necessarily share the same experiences. I also often find that assumptions/tropes about diaspora are projected onto me.'

I don't want to discard the identity of 'diaspora', as that can dismiss the hard and dedicated work of independence that colonial states fought for. As a result of that fight, we have a place 'to come from', and it is a term that still feels the best fit for me. But so many of us intimately know this land of Britain sometimes better than our own. As someone who grew up in a settler state, I see how it mimicked the green pastures of England so that I yearned for a landscape that I had never met. And even with my knowledge of colonialism, which I was lucky to have been taught about from a young age, I was still drawn to this story of the UK as motherland. It was the place to be educated in, the path to a better future.

On why she came to the UK to finish high school, Vera said: 'I felt like I was a bit of an alien in Malaysian society, probably because my mother was an Anglophile. My parents were both educated by the British, and had gone to England as part of the first wave of teachers being trained here and so they're very entrenched in the "British education system is the best in the world", "Marks & Spencer is an icon" rhetoric.' It was far from ideal for Vera to finish their higher education in Malaysia, because of the barriers ethnic Chinese faced in higher education, on top of the focus on British education being the only education worth having. Vera knew her parents wouldn't be able to afford to send her to England, but there was a school fair and, at sixteen, Vera took her CV around the different stalls. 'I pimped myself out – I guess an overachieving Malaysian looks great on paper compared to the English standard.' She was determined to go. Vera convinced a school to create a scholarship that funded 75 per cent of her school fees and boarding, and, somehow, her parents found the rest.

'I was watching the Royal Shakespeare Company (RSC) do Shakespeare on VHS tapes. My mother [an English teacher] would make me illustrate idioms and read the pronunciation dictionary. I had tons and tons of not only English books, but English comics from the 1960s and 1970s. Not only was I reading Enid Blyton but I saw pop culture – miniskirts and hot [white] boys – and I felt very much like "how can I possibly stay in Malaysia?" ' Vera said.

British identity is so dominant in our postcolonial psyche that 'you feel like it's a country that is above us,' my London-based friend and actor Safiah Durrah explains to me when talking about her perception of the UK when growing up in Malaysia. 'There is still this belief that it's much more superior, that you would go to the UK to study, that's it's a better education than what you would receive in Malaysia. Now I understand there are really talented professionals and artists that were born, bred and educated in Malaysia.'

Filipino chef Mae Williams told me how she arrived in Sevenoaks, Kent at the age of fourteen with her sister, joining her mother who was the housekeeper for a Danish family. 'Before leaving [the] Philippines, my impression of the UK was that it was a good country to study, picturesque scenery and people are lovely, that studying in the UK would open doors for me for my future.'

For KG Patarita Tassanarapan, a Thai chef and artist, education was also the driving force for her to come to the UK, pursuing a master's degree in fine arts. 'I choose to study here because it's my dream to study at the Architectural Association School of Architecture. I knew a few people who had graduated from this school, they were impressively creative and critical. So I bet that an education from the AA, as well as the environment of the city of London, must reinforce the individual's intellect and growth.' She didn't see herself as an artist before coming to the UK, but studying and living here meant that she was able to develop and find her practice.

I asked Jenny why she is here. 'I am here because my parents were really smart. Both my parents came from big families and were the "smartest" of the siblings, spoke very good English, got the grades that enabled them to get scholarships to study abroad or be recruited by the NHS.' The smart ones go to Europe to study; the colonial project of devaluing ourselves and our heritage knowledge worked successfully. And, Jenny reminds me, 'we tend to forget that immigrants – sorry* – are the ones who successfully make it abroad. Think about all the factors involved in making such a move, especially mid-twentieth century!'

As a way to rethink about their relationship to diaspora,

---

* 'I think it's interesting that we have a tendency to interchange "migrant" and "immigrant", but the greatest tension is when we choose to use "expat". The former two can have pejorative connotations; the latter tends to be afforded to the white and privileged. I think we can resist this racialisation of "immigrant" versus "expat" by insisting that everyone living outside their native country is an expat,' Jenny explains when discussing the importance of language in reframing ourselves.

both Vera and Jenny lean into the idea of 'immigrant'. 'I like the specificity of using generational terms. For example, if someone says they are "second-generation British Cantonese" versus a recent "Cantonese immigrant", a well-informed person can already start to build a picture about those two people's personal histories, socio-economic backgrounds and migration motivations. You can probably pinpoint where in Hong Kong or which clan they came from. But at what point do you stop saying the "immigrant" bit and just say . . . "British"?' Jenny says.

'I tend to use the word "immigrant" and I specify "first-generation immigrant to the UK" because the length of stay is significant,' Vera says. 'Ironically, I only started using the term "immigrant" *after* I wrote "Yellow" for *The Good Immigrant** and had one of those "oh shit" moments realising that I *am* an immigrant, with all the accompanying baggage.

'Furthermore, I think it's significant in terms of granularity that I came over on my own, not with my family, i.e. we did not emigrate here with the force and foresight of planning; I am a first-gen immigrant on my own,' she explains to me.

My migration story feels like a jumble of lines criss-crossing the world. I was born mere weeks after my father had finished his PhD in Australia and was whisked away back to Sarawak. My memories of my childhood are

---

* *The Good Immigrant* is a collection of essays published in 2016 and edited by Nikesh Shukla, for which Vera wrote the essay 'Yellow'.

wonderful: travelling upriver in a longboat with my dad on the campaign trail. He became a politician in 1983, setting up the first Indigenous party. Like many of his generation, the dreams of a new world were exciting. He and his contemporaries were in a position to really shape the future of their new country and state; it was only two decades since independence. I remember telling my mother I hated being half white. I spoke Iban and don't remember ever being treated differently, but I wanted to be part of the norm – fully Sarawakian.

When my parents divorced, my sister Rachel and I moved to Auckland, New Zealand with my mother. The winter we arrived in 1988, Cyclone Bola hit. I remember struggling up the street through the wind and rain and being baffled by the weather. I was put in the lowest reading group, despite having read all the books, as my dyslexia was not understood. I remember someone yelling at me for being Samoan. I could tell by the tone that this kid thought that was an insult, but I didn't understand why it would be an insult, and also, I *wasn't* Samoan. It was the only 'other' he had been taught about, at age six. I remember I was told I spoke 'funny', and so I lost my Malaysian accent within two weeks. The idea of 'other' was beginning to form. But I have a really strong sense of being Iban, which I can only attribute to my mother. She taught me how to be Iban, Malaysian, Asian. Not through details, but through remembrance and stories and food.

A lot of my time in New Zealand was happy, but I was constantly adrift. I look back now and see the passive-aggressive racism, the constant microaggressions, the 'Asians are X, no offence,' and 'but not you, I don't mean you, you're different'. People always say they were shocked to hear about the racist Christchurch mosque shootings in 2019, because New Zealanders 'are so nice', but it didn't surprise me at all. There was always a seething underbelly of othering and I felt it keenly. New Zealand has never felt like home. As soon as I finished high school, I went to live with my dad for four months, got an Iban tattoo designed by an Iban tattooist, interned for the Sarawak tourism board and made some really great friends. I went back to Auckland, started a degree in English and Art History, but I knew I wanted to be in London, in Britain. I wanted to go on bejalai – an Iban coming-of-age travelling ritual. I wanted to be away from New Zealand. My dad asked me to write a business proposal for why he should pay for me to study in the UK, and I chose a degree that interested me the most: performing arts at London Metropolitan University. I wish I could remember my business angle on this, no doubt a combination of naivety and a promise to work really, really hard.

I arrived in London on 4 September 2001, under a Labour government. I watched the Twin Towers collapse on a small TV in my flatmate's room seven days later. My university had the highest racial diversity and most first-in-their-family-in-higher-education students in the whole of the country. It was on Holloway Road, which was almost central London. It was busy and I loved it. I wanted to go to protests against the Iraq War in 2003 but was too scared about what that would mean for my visa. How would authorities – the police, the state – treat me if I got arrested?

After I finished my undergraduate degree, I got a two-year working visa. Only people with New Zealand, South African, Australian and Canadian – white settler states – passports had access to this. The year I applied, there were no restrictions on how many months I needed to spend working or travelling, so I worked full time. I fell in love with a Greek Australian who had a Greek passport. We married at twenty-four and I got a spousal visa. The process of visas is complicated, intimidating and the information purposefully difficult to find. I once got my student visa denied because in the two-day time period from printing out the forms to filling them in, the forms had changed but there was no information on the website. I once queued from 4 a.m. at the Home Office to get a visa renewal. My sister Rachel was visiting, so I was lucky to have her with me – but I felt we were physically vulnerable doing that, on a dark winter morning in a part of London we didn't know.

I got my British citizenship and passport in 2013. I dressed up in blue, red and white, and I swore allegiance to the Queen. My mum and a very pregnant Rachel were there and we went out for lunch afterwards. I ordered a salmon salad at Ottolenghi's on Upper Street, Islington.

I have lived in London longer, by far, than anywhere else. It has been my entire adult life. It has always felt like home, from the moment I arrived. I can't imagine being anywhere else. I loved it from that first week of university – trying to decipher a Barnsley accent, learning that spunk was *not* how to describe a hot guy, and being surrounded by so much difference.

But I still feel desperately nervous writing my immigration story here, in public, in case I did something wrong and it will all be taken away from me. Immigration law is designed to alienate, to dehumanise, to other. The work of othering that colonialism did, that empire thrived on, has fed into immigration policy. The white settler states, to uphold their identities as 'other Englands',[25] created racialised policies that are being enacted and reinterpreted now in the UK. The link between the acts of empire is seen in our immigration systems. This chapter has been extremely difficult to write because every word I chose means I am discarding other stories, other experiences, other policies and rulings and concepts of borders. Empire and migration are extremely complex and messy. And as diaspora, as immigrants, as third culture kids, our legitimacy in this space is bound in these histories.

Chapter 3

Violence

It is dangerous to live in non-white bodies. To be recognisable as East or South East Asian on the streets of Britain is to live in peril.

A report published in April 2022 by Sandy Schumann and Ysanne Moore of the Department of Security and Crime Science at University College London framed the outbreak of the Covid-19 pandemic as a 'trigger event' for East Asian hate speech, where spikes in online Sinophobic language in the UK increased.[1] They looked at the period between January 2020 and March 2020, when the first cases were recorded in China, a time when Donald Trump called Covid-19 the 'Chinese Virus'.

They note that it is hard to analyse the data from the police records (such as from the Metropolitan Police), as racist and religious hate crimes are grouped together in one category, which includes anti-Semitic, Islamophobic, faith hate crime and race hate crime. But, from May 2020, incidents in this category did increase, and in conjunction with a victimisation survey to capture experiences that weren't able to be captured by police, Schumann and Moore were able to draw some clear conclusions.

The months directly after the first cases of Covid-19 were reported in the UK contained the highest level of hate crime against those from 'Chinese and East Asian'* backgrounds. These incidents were more likely to occur in public spaces, and to be verbal harassment. One of the major issues with gathering this data is the way the data is segmented by the police. The term 'Asian' represents such a wide grouping of people in the UK that it proved difficult to be effectively clear about what was an East and/or South East Asian hate crime, and therefore what may be have been a pandemic-related incident. The other issue is to do with reporting. Although Schumann and Moore explain that abuse was most likely to happen offline, online harassment is not often viewed as a crime, and therefore is not likely to be reported, making it difficult to include it in figures. This means that a full statistical picture of the race violence perpetuated during the pandemic is tricky to gauge.

'We shed light on the scale of Anti-East Asian hate in the United Kingdom and, in doing so, emphasize the need to record official ethnic and race crime data at a more granular level,' conclude the authors. Nuance is needed, as are categories that aren't just Asian; or Chinese, or Any Other Asian.

---

* This report looks at Anti-East Asian hate crime, or at least is defining Sinophobia as such. It is unclear if they would include South East Asian victims who have been perceived as Chinese and/ or East Asian; anecdotally I know a lot people of South East Asian heritage who also experienced Covid-19 related abuse.

As well as being on the frontline of heightened racism and/or having a heightened awareness of being racialised during this time, ESEA people were also reading news about how those of ethnic minority backgrounds were more likely to die or be severely ill from Covid-19. Public Health England published a report in August 2020 stating 'death rates from Covid-19 were highest amongst people of Black and Asian ethnic groups'. Those of Bangladeshi ethnicity were at twice the risk of death compared to White British, and 'people of Chinese, Indian, Pakistani, Other Asian, Black Caribbean and Other Black ethnicity had between 10 and 50 per cent higher risk of death when compared to White British.'[2] In June 2020, the *Nursing Times* reported that the International Council of Nurses were concerned at the high death rate of Philippine nurses in the NHS.[3] Written evidence submitted to the Filipino Nurses Association UK stated that by May 2020, 22 per cent of all NHS staff deaths had been those of Filipino background. Filipino healthcare workers make up just 3.8 per cent of the NHS staff. It felt like every day there was a story about how people like us were constantly in harm's way. It felt systematic, it was systematic.

These incidents are not statistics. They are personal, they are people in our communities.

John and Yee Li are a husband-and-wife team who own the popular London-based food group Dumpling Shack, with three sites across the city. Both are British-born Chinese, and have a long history in the restaurant industry. John's parents moved to the UK from Hong Kong as teenagers, and worked in John's paternal grandfather's restaurant in Hounslow, a suburb in Greater London. His parents then opened a Chinese restaurant, Caterham Chinese Restaurant, in 1984 in Surrey, where John spent his teenage years working. It is now owned by his sister. John studied law, then worked in the banking industry, before founding his own restaurant group. Yee's parents had a Chinese takeaway in Cheshunt, Hertfordshire, also not far from London. Similarly, she worked in the banking industry before meeting John and the pair started Dumpling Shack.

On 29 March 2021, John posted on Dumpling Shack's Instagram profile about how Yee and he had been walking through Canary Wharf when they were spat at. 'I have never felt like more of a second class citizen and I have today [sic],' he wrote. In the video, he explains how there was nothing he could do, how any reactive violence would get him in trouble and that he worries about when lockdown lifts. 'Wait until more of society starts interacting, starts to lose more inhibitions.' He continues in the post's caption with: 'We can't do anything more to be part of this country, we're born here, we created jobs, we pay a ton of tax, (it's an eye watering amount), we support charities in this country [...] but we won't be beat. Fuck that, im doubling down, working even harder and making our presence even more known. WE'RE NOT GOING ANYWHERE.' John followed the two men, filming their backs, and asked them, 'Did you spit at me?' The men ignore him.[4]

To spit on someone is a violent act. It invades physical space, with bodily fluid, which makes it a deeply personal attack. It is a universal sign of disrespect and disgust. To spit on someone in the UK is considered a criminal offence and is classed as common assault. To spit on someone during a pandemic where a virus is spread through droplets ejected from the mouth and nose makes it a possibly deadly act. I tell this story because John and Yee are my friends and they've given me permission to do so. I have quoted from the Instagram post because I think it's important to know that they made this act public, and I think they were bold and brave in doing so. But these stories became so familiar to me over the pandemic and to many in the ESEA community. If it didn't happen to you, it happened to someone you knew.

The Schumann and Moore report refers to East Asian hate crimes, because the pandemic reporting in the West focused attention on China, which became conflated with Chinese people. But this 'anti East Asian' sentiment and violence was not restricted to ethnically Chinese people alone. The identity of East and South East Asian people has been merged as one, through language, policy, histories, systematic othering and lack of understanding. People were on the receiving end of racist violence if the perpetrator perceived them as being *possibly* Chinese. But this racism didn't start with Covid-19, the pandemic simply gave it an excuse. In July 2020, the Commission of Countering Extremism published a report stating a recent rise in extremism and 'anti-minority narratives', and that far-right groups were exploiting the pandemic to justify attacks for a myriad of reasons.[5] As John points out in his post, the pandemic gave a space for people to lose inhibitions.

As journalist Georgina Phuong My Quach, who is of Vietnamese heritage, explains to me, 'the outbreak of Covid forced a harsh spotlight on the ESEA community. I feared and still fear that many non-ESEA people see this type of racism as contained within the Covid pandemic, by misguided people, and not [as it is] the secondary effect of a long history of prejudice, distrust, and hatred against ESEA folks – for which scapegoating of ESEA people as vectors of the virus is a devastating consequence. Many of us have experienced ESEA racism all our lives, in so many forms and even by those who don't even realise it.' Georgina explained how a year before Covid-19, she was spat on in her hometown.

It isn't only physical and obvious racism. It is also about silencing or a refusal for East and South East Asian stories of violence to be heard and witnessed unless they are sensational. 'I remember months after the Atlanta shooting,* and months after the flurry of protests in the UK and US against anti-Asian violence, I pitched

---

* On 16 March 2021, eight people were killed, six of which were women of East and/or South East Asian descent, by a 21-year-old white man who claimed that he was motivated by a sexual addiction. The killings happened at spas and massage parlours. This incident prompted 'Stop Asian Hate' demonstrations across the US, as well as rallying solidarity in UK.

a story on anti-ESEA violence to a national newspaper. It was turned down, as there was no "news hook", no attention-grabbing deaths in Britain to speak of. What kind of message does this send to those of us who have survived racial violence both during and outside of the pandemic?' Georgina asks.

Sarah Owen, the Labour MP who is of mixed Chinese Malaysian heritage and white British, told me that when she first started high school, a girl who was sat behind her made comments and pulled her eyes to the side. A few years later, that teenage girl brought a knife to school and threatened to kill Sarah because she didn't believe in the mixing of races. There are many ways this incident can be brushed off as unusual, but this teenage girl will have learnt this narrative from somewhere and have had it reinforced within public spaces. Bullying left unchecked and narratives left unchallenged can be very dangerous.

In October 2020, Sarah proposed a parliamentary discussion in relation to the rise in hate crime against Chinese people and communities. As part of this proposal, she demonstrated that at least a third of stories related to Covid-19 across UK publications used imagery with East and South East Asian faces as their subjects. This research was done by End the Virus of Racism* and Britain's East and South East Asian Network, who analysed 14,000 images across fifteen major news outlets from January

---

* Now renamed EVR: End Violence and Racism Against East and Southeast Asian Communities.

2020 to August 2020.[6] If we only see stories of violence on Asian bodies in the media, without contextualising how this violence is processed, and how it is linked to a deadly pandemic, then we are bodies reduced to news hooks. This is an othering that enables great harm. It reduces us to simple, two-dimensional beings, or simply statistics.

This isn't the first time, not even in recent history, that the media has helped in perpetuating racism with devastating effect with regards to a virus. In 2001, Chinese restaurants were wrongly accused of being the origin of a terrible outbreak of foot and mouth disease in the UK, which the British press ran with despite the lack of evidence. This caused verbal and physical abuse in public and in Chinese takeaways and restaurants, as well as the vandalising of those businesses. Chinese businesses lost approximately £24 million in income.[7] These narratives, such as with Covid-19 and foot and mouth, where East Asians, and at times specifically Chinese people, are blamed or scapegoated are all echoes of Victorian rhetoric, the Dickensian descriptions of opium dens with disreputable characters, that are repeated in the early twentieth century with plays and literature about 'Yellow Peril'. And, of course, when a newspaper gets a story wrong, they don't print the correction on the front page. The narrative stays in the public perception, mostly uncontested.

Writer and journalist Angela Hui has been writing about ESEA food, culture and voices for many years. In March 2021, she wrote for Refinery29 about how she cried and cried, every time, reading and seeing images of

ESEA hate crimes that kept pouring in across news sites from across the global north during the pandemic.[8] These were images of people who looked like our loved ones. In the introduction to her 2022 book, *Takeaway: Stories from a Childhood Behind the Counter*, Angela writes 'the attacks that are happening now validate my long-held suspicions of racism towards ESEA people, backing up the tales of my family fending off drunk, racist customers and vandalism attacks on our shop. Coronavirus has only sharpened this inchoate prejudice and renamed it "kung flu".'[9] Angela said to me that writing and publishing this book during the pandemic was difficult and isolating, but ultimately felt important and bigger than herself alone. 'I felt I was doing something important to me – telling my story and my family's story, and just needed to get words down on paper – but also with the Asian hate and anti-Chinese sentiment around Covid, we needed to have [our] stories heard more than ever.' She felt, in contrast to the US, there wasn't a huge coming together and rallying, such as support for Chinatowns and Chinese restaurants, because we are a more disparate community, making us less heard. But she reflects that there has been an 'explosion' of books and stories since the pandemic, proving there is an appetite for our stories, which is exciting and needed. It is our stories that can change wider cultural narratives.

In August 2021, I wrote a piece on celebrating ESEA women in the food industry for Resy London, on the editorial side of the restaurant booking site. It consisted of four interviews with different women: chefs, writers, community organisers. I was lucky that the editor was David Paw, London-based international editor of Resy (where it was published), who is Burmese-born and of Karen heritage; he wanted to highlight the heightened awareness of ESEA racism due to Covid-19, the effects of racism and racist systems, and also to shine a light on the work that these women had been doing, to celebrate them. David was very clear that we should show joy while telling the stories of trauma, because joy is a radical act when you are being marginalised and subjected to violence.

'In the immediate aftermath of Atlanta the feeling was "How can we not talk about this? How can we talk about anything else?" For months, every moment felt run through with the pain of women in the broad Asian community who had experienced this very specific form of sexualised racism and violence throughout their lives. You and I and everyone we knew were palpably hurting, and sharing these stories was hopefully a source of insight and awareness while being an outlet for the individuals you spoke to,' David said to me.

Haein Park,* a chef of South Korean heritage who has lived in the US, UK and India, explained to me how much the Atlanta shootings had affected her. She wished she had surrounded herself with more ESEA women to build a network of checking in with each other. She also expressed the point that so much activism and public

---

* A pseudonym.

response within the UK's ESEA community against the hate, harassment and violence had come from women. What is crucial here is also how often this isn't seen or even recognised as work. These violent stories, such as the Atlanta shootings – which may seem to others so far away, both in location and likelihood of happening – are close to home because they remind us that we are othered. The Atlanta shootings reminded us how othering is violent, how even the smallest microaggression sits on the edge of violence, and how physically unsafe we can be. But in particular, this incident was at the intersection of gender and race. Haein's response reminded me how much we, as women, had to rely on ourselves and each other. During those months, I left many teary voice notes to other women.

It is easy to understand physical abuse and hate-filled sentences as racism, but it is important to address dealing with more than just physical or verbal violence. When we can see how and when the violence lands – on our skin, in our ears – we can understand the harm it causes. It is harder to understand when it is subtle, small moments of discomfort – microaggressions. But these are violent too. They add up to create a world that is hostile, a continued eradication of self and a sense of belonging.

The term 'microaggression' was coined in the 1970s by US psychiatrist Dr Chester M. Pierce, in which he referred to the idea of 'racial microaggression' with particular reference to African Americans. It is important to note that this term began as a way of understanding the effects of racialised aggression. Micro is in reference to the size of the aggression, and that it is often perceived by the aggressor as inoffensive or at least insignificant. A 2019 paper produced by Natasha N. Johnson and Thasseus Johnson for Georgia State University's Department of Criminal Justice and Criminology titled *Microaggressions: An Introduction* gives some of the best explanations and definitions of the term I have seen. They say it is 'in no way, however, "micro" in that the potentially detrimental impact it bears on the victims can be lasting and down-right hurtful.' Although these aggressions lack the threat of physical harm, Johnson and Johnson explain '[s]imilar to an assault, microaggressions can produce fear, stress, and emotional harm, and may embarrass or intimidate the victim, undermine his or her credibility, and expose vulnerabilities.'[10] Microaggressions can include things like being mistaken for another East or South East Asian person in the office, assumed to be of a heritage you are not, or a disparaging comment made about your culture in your presence.

Lisa, my Vietnamese Australian friend who works in IT, has found real belonging in London. She thinks that the vast array of Asian-ness that is represented in the UK is interesting and inspiring, compared to growing up in Australia. 'There's more vocabulary and awareness of it these days; in the 1980s in Australia, there was no language for it, so it was just isolated misery,' she says. At many points over the last thirteen years of living in London, her friends have been either all or majority ESEA. But she still notices the disdain and casual racism, for example, towards chefs of ESEA background. 'It's not funny to mock the accent but say you love the food.' She tells me a story of a chain restaurant that had Vietnamese 'inspired' coffees. 'I emailed them to let them know that's not a Vietnamese coffee. They answered saying – yes, it's just "inspired" by it.' This sort of brush off seems so small, but it was hurtful as it was a dismissal of both her personal knowledge and also the idea that her culture can just be *used* without care and as fodder for lazy 'inspiration', with no background or context. This casualness is reiterated daily and in small 'micro' moments, and is exhausting.

The only way the racism experienced in a heightened period, such as with Covid-19, won't happen again is if we radically change the way we are seen. I speak of 'we' in multiples here – we as society as a whole, the social and political structure of our society and country, and we as being part of ESEA people. It is vital that our ESEA stories are told in multiple spaces, with a sense of multiple and complex identities.

Through the period of rising hate crime during the Covid-19 pandemic, particularly in 2020, verbal abuse was most common, as Schumann and Moore point out. I therefore want to reinforce the importance of language and its connection to violence. We need to understand that racialisation is important and to recognise that it was Chinese-ness that was being targeted. Violence against other East and South East Asian groups was often collateral. Scholar and literary theorist Shu-mei Shih coined

the phrase 'Sinophone' in 2004 as a way to look at literature and culture written 'on the margins of China and
Chineseness'.[11] This lens investigates ideas of empire (both
European and Chinese), colonialism, nostalgia and the
need to decentre and encompass the periphery in relation
to Sinophone culture.

By looking at the complexity of what it means to be
Chinese, we can understand how language plays a part in
creating structures of violence, and we can also begin to
rethink our understanding of diaspora and indeed migration. This is about making complex the idea of identity,
so that people aren't seen as categories and therefore easily
oppressed or harmed.

We can think about migration as a form of cultural
movement, where influences develop and shift across the
world. It isn't as simple as saying that groups of Chinese
people moved from China to Malaysia, and then from
Malaysia to the UK. Identities develop as people engage
with the space they move to and 'place' becomes a part
of new identities. As Shu-mei Shih writes, 'Sinophone
Malaysian writers, for instance, often incorporate English,
Malay, and Tamil into their work, not to mention often
crossing different Sinitic languages such as Mandarin,
Hokkien, and Cantonese.'[12] When I have travelled in
Malaysia with British Chinese Malaysian friends Vera
Chok and Mandy Yin (on separate trips), their ability
to speak Malay was crucial in us getting around. By
taking away the specificity of time, space and journeys,
we eradicate a sense of identity and evolving traditions. In

the UK, we see one Chinese identity through Peranakan* food cultures in our Singaporean and Malaysian restaurants. The Peranakan identity is sometimes told as a story dating back to the 1400s, of a Chinese princess, a Sultan of Malacca and Chinese traders, but is mainly agreed to be relating to the migration of mostly Southern mainland Chinese men to the Straits of Malacca in the nineteenth century who then married local women.

Tan Chee-Beng discusses the idea of Chinese diaspora in his 2004 book, *Chinese Overseas: Comparative Cultural Issues*, and writes 'when we compare Chinese cultures in China to Chinese cultures overseas, we do not see this as a relationship of the centre to the periphery. In the Chinese ethnological field, each Chinese "society" is its own cultural centre.' He goes on to explain that cultural practices in China are also influenced by Chinese in diaspora and/ or communities of Chinese descent in other countries – the flow of influence is dynamic, back and forth, and of multiples. Indeed, the term of 'Chinese diaspora' is one that is contested, as Tan points out, because the idea of centre is troubled when thinking about Chinese migration.[13] Diaspora is generally related to a specific regional space, often a nation state. This is all-important because it helps us understand how the simplistic language of

---

* Chinese Peranakan are also known as Strait Chinese. Not all Peranakan are of Chinese heritage, there are Malay Peranakan and even a small group of Indian Peranakan known as Chitty Melaka, whose heritage is related to Tamil traders from the fifteenth century onwards.

the media, Donald Trump or UK politicians eradicates personal nuance and works to make ESEA hate legitimate. It condenses people into one identity, such as a state.

When rhetoric against China as a state is used, it can be problematic and might potentially lead to violence, such as during the pandemic. During the UK Conservative party leadership campaign in the summer of 2022, Rishi Sunak tweeted on 25 July that 'China and the Chinese Communist Party represent the largest threat to Britain.'[14] The thread included plans to shut down Mandarin language teaching in the UK, with claims that some of the institutions that taught it were promoting soft power, and scaremongering around hacking, disregarding the idea of people learning a language to develop connections to their historical ancestral language, or learning about a culture through its language. 'We have been too soft on China. I won't be,' Penny Mordaunt tweeted on 19 July, without context or definition.[15] This language conflates people and culture with state, a purposeful act to create fear and an 'other' to be fearful of. This language is an echo of Trump's 'China Virus' comment two and a half years earlier in the context of Covid-19. These are bookends of the pandemic stoking fear; conspiracy notions that have real life consequences.

With this, an environment is built where racism seems like a justified act, by creating an origin or centre: 'China', to which certain people can be pinned to. Georgina, the journalist, and I sent texts back and forth about these tweets at the time – with fury and simply 'ugh'.

Georgina further says to me, 'China itself is a huge country with a vast variety of languages, cultures, climates and political viewpoints. Still, in the UK, those distinctions are generally erased in mainstream consciousness and we are all treated as "Chinese" (as long as you "look" East Asian). So a lot of us face the consequences of Sinophobia, and the reality is that the constant conflation of China (state) with China (families, humans, dreams) ends up perpetuating all of us as the "other" and the peril which must be subdued.'

These simplistic representations of a space, such as China, erases individual experiences of place, culture and family. Georgina's grandmother is ethnically Chinese but lived in Vietnam, as did both of her parents. 'My immediate family is probably more Vietnamese in spirit and culture – particularly in terms of being part of a national narrative of resettlement. But we enjoy a freedom and flexibility to express ourselves in multiple ESEA cultural vocabularies.' Georgina grew up absorbing four languages at home: Vietnamese, Chiu Chow, Cantonese and English. At the dinner table, her family would flit between all these languages, even within a single sentence. 'Going for yum cha [eating dim sum with relatives] feels like a Cantonese family tradition and it is generally where I pick up Cantonese phrases and words, but it's very much part of our [Vietnamese] story too.'

Georgina's story demonstrates this idea of having multiple identities and cultural heritage, which cannot be contained into a single regional or notion of state.

She told me about growing up in Milton Keynes: '[It] was not exactly a fertile ground for probing questions about race and racism, and the only Vietnamese people I knew were my family. Its reputation as a town is associated with cultural blankness and grey, linear landscapes. Somehow there is a forgiving, misguided attitude to those who poke fun at other cultures and races – young people who were racist towards me are seen as just unexposed or uneducated, so I felt a lot of guilt and internalised prejudice.' She tells me that her friends who grew up in London appreciated a curiosity of others, rather than fearing it. But she was shaped by this experience, and left open to influences and finding nourishment: 'It was up to me to fill in the blanks.'

Georgina moved to Oxford, then Sheffield, for her undergraduate and postgraduate university studies, moving from one white-dominated space to another. She studied English Literature at the University of Oxford, reading some of the oldest texts by Anglo-Saxons and the forefathers of poetry. 'Yet on the other hand, I had to swallow a lot of racial prejudice and assumptions by some members of the public outside of the university community – "How do you speak English so well? Did you do karate when you were a kid? Are you from China?" ' She explains that her personal exploration of her heritage was held back at both institutions, because they approached race and racism in a top-down fashion. She found Oxford used race as a political tool, 'where "liberal" debates were excited by political movement rather than care, sharing

food or the untold trauma of peoples' heritage'. She strug-
gled to find writing avenues that focused on individuals,
the complexity of knowing and belonging to multiple
cultures which is also about patterns of resettlement and
'being transplanted in a foreign country. I remember I
tried to write about [race through] my family recipes for a
publication – with a white male editor – and they weren't
convinced by the idea. It was incredibly hard and stopped
me from properly trying again,' she said.

Taking away the personal experience means that structures that oppress and/or 'other' cannot be understood
with any nuance. It also allows for inequality to not be
properly interrogated. To discuss is not to change. The
lack of care devoted to the everyday actions and routines
renders the individual, the family, the community hidden.
By focusing solely on race as political and structural, we
then play into the conflation that politicians and the
like can manipulate and we – ESEA people – become a
monolith. In Chapter 6, I'll discuss the issue of taking the
political out of discussions on food. It makes the discussion and work on equality shallow, and stops debates on
race from moving forward. We have to find a way to
have room for both the personal and the political in these
conversations.

By taking into account the personal stories and traject-
ories, we are then able to understand and investigate full
intersections of identity. And class is crucial when discussing race. Within discussions of working-class people,

race often gets left out of the conversation and yet they go hand in hand. As much as, or sometimes even more so than race, class affects the spaces you have access to and the confidence with which you move through those spaces.

The intersection of class and race can be a violent one; it has violent repercussions if an identity gets diminished into something small and expendable. Those that are particularly vulnerable are new migrants, especially those who are undocumented and/or working low-income jobs, who might not have access to services or have barriers, such as language, that make it difficult to advocate for themselves. In February 2004, twenty-three Chinese* men and women drowned in Morecambe Bay as they harvested cockles. These people were undocumented migrants, and the tragedy exposed a dark side to the food industry where vulnerable people where trafficked into the UK as cheap labour. The Lancashire Police also reported other industries, including nail salons and sex work, used Chinese migrants who had taken similar routes into the UK. After the Morecambe Bay disaster, the Gangmasters and Labour Abuse Authority (GLAA)† was set up in aid of finding ways to 'protect vulnerable and exploited workers'. In 2011, the Joseph Rowntree Foundation, an organisation that aims to end poverty

---

* ITV reported that most of the victims were from the Fujian Province in China. [16]

† Originally named the Gangmasters Licensing Authority (GLA).

in the UK, conducted a research project, interviewing thirty-three people of Chinese origins working in low-paying, labour-intensive jobs. This research demonstrated persistent exploitive work conditions, where '[e]mployers flouted immigration and employment regulations to make use of cheap, flexible labour'.[17] The stories highlighted exhaustion, fear, intimidation and barriers for getting help, such as language and access to information.

Research conducted by the Business and Human Rights Resource Centre in 2023[18] looked into abuse in the care sector in the global north and showed women from the Philippines and India being the most impacted, and that the UK had the most violations (65 per cent). In October 2023, the UK's Modern Slavery and Exploitation Helpline operator, Unseen, reported that there was a 606 per cent increase in modern slavery cases in the care sector in a year (2021–2022).[19] A Business and Human Rights Resource Centre publication wrote that a key issue with migrant workers was 'financial control, such as by withholding wages, not paying the minimum wage, debt bondage and charging excessive fees for breaking contracts',[20] and a parliamentary report in 2022 showed that zero contract hours are more common in the care sector than any other. There are reports of recruitment, visa and travel fees and even allegations of UK care companies incorporating recruitments fees into business models.[21] With visas tied to work, there is fear of complaining leading to losing jobs, which would leave the workers with irregular status. A report by UNISON in 2023 highlighted in detail the abuse received in the care sector and described it as systemic. It points out that although the ill-treatment is 'rife' throughout the sector, 'unscrupulous employers have greater powers over migrant care workers, which leads to the most extreme and disgraceful practices'.[22]

These stories of exploitation are often framed as an issue with bad players – the gangs that traffic people, the employers – all of whom are important to evaluate, but this approach also hides the systemic issue with exploiting migrants. It isn't just individuals conducting criminal behaviour but rather a system that needs cheap labour, and keeps abuse and violence hidden. Immigration and labour laws create areas of vulnerability, the economics of capitalism strive for cheap labour, and it means that people in the working classes, historically and continuously, are denied rights; these people are predominantly new migrants of colour, where visa status can be a tool for manipulation.

Post-Brexit, unique visa schemes were introduced for seasonal workers (agricultural sector) and the care sector, and although this has provided specific entry into the UK, the process has been left open for abuse. In March 2024, the Modern Slavery and Human Rights Policy and Evidence Centre, a consortium led by the University of Oxford, published research showing that the agriculture and care worker industries were particularly vulnerable; this report included support from Southeast and East Asian Centre and Kanlungan Filipino Consortium. The report says these visas 'exacerbate migrant agriculture and care workers' precarious position', citing low wages and high recruitment fees. The report also describes how the 'Hostile/Complaint Environment'* policies were key in allowing abuse to happen.[23] These policies were put in place in 2012 by Theresa May while she was home secretary, and make complaining about unfair situations feel impossible, as it could jeopardise work hours that would affect visa status. Abuse of migrant workers is not a recent phenomenon: May's 2012 policies will have decades-long repercussions, the Morecambe Bay tragedy happened over twenty years ago, and in 2000, fifty-eight Chinese people were killed, suffocating to death in a lorry at Dover. If we keep looking back, we will find many stories; this paints a picture of the violence of exploitation.

In 2009, research was conducted by The Monitoring Group,† an anti-racism organisation, on racism against the Chinese population in the UK from early 2007 to early 2008. The racism experienced by research participants included racist name-calling, property damage (such as

---

*   This is a set of 2012 policies that were implemented by the then Home Secretary Theresa May, which aimed to make living in the UK as a migrant 'unbearable'. I recommend this report from The Joint Council for the Welfare of Immigrants: The Hostile Environment Explained (https://jcwi.org.uk/reportsbriefings/the-hostile-environment-explained/) as a starting point to understanding the impact.

†   The research was part of their Min Quan project, which was established to help victims of racism and hate crimes in the British Chinese community. The report included authors from the University of Hull, University of Leeds and Nottingham Trent University.

arson and physical attacks that led to hospitalisation) and murder – racism is violence.

The report was dedicated to Mi Gao Huang Chen, who was murdered on 23 April 2005 when he was attacked by over twenty white youths outside his takeaway restaurant in Lancashire. The report explained that in the aftermath of this murder, although having had experience supporting families of murdered victims, such as those of Stephen Lawrence, Victoria Climbié and Zahid Mubarek, 'it took a major and concerted effort to force the investigation [of Mi Gao Huang Chen] and prosecution agencies to work with the victim group and take our concerns seriously'. It cites that most of the criticism of the criminal justice system by Chinese people was against the police, and it continued to demonstrate how official policies, processes or systems are not trusted and/or able to deal with the racial abuse received by the Chinese community in the UK. This report was titled 'Hidden from public view?', and encapsulates how violence in the ESEA communities is often not acknowledged, seen or listened to. This report interviewed predominantly people in the catering industry, but also interviewed people with other careers and statuses, such as students and the unemployed, and specifically points to systematic marginalisation: 'the report shows that Chinese-origin people in the UK experience substantial racism, perhaps as much as or more than any other minority ethnic group yet, because of the way in which statistics are collected and presented, and because of the response in practice of most public agencies, this experience is hidden from public view.'[24]

At the beginning of this chapter, we discussed that the ability to record accurately, because of a homogenisation of 'Asian', means that properly understanding the scope of violence for ESEA communities – which is one that includes the intersection of class – is hidden and therefore impossible to investigate, support and change. This study was also clear that it spoke to Chinese people from different countries, acknowledging the complexity of the Chinese identity, and showcases how in-depth, intersectional research can understand violence and look towards nuanced solutions.

Class does shift, and can be viewed differently in different spaces. Lisa was born in a Vietnamese refugee camp in Malaysia in the late 1970s. When she and her parents arrived in Sydney, her parents worked low-paying menial jobs and split childcare between them – one worked day-shifts, the other worked nights. Lisa was the first in her family to go to university. Her education and Australian passport become something different in the UK: 'I'm the "right" kind of immigrant. Aussie Asian is better than Asian-Asian. As an Aussie, I'm familiar/more relatable than someone who has a [non-English speaking] accent. Less effort is needed on their part. Hearing English people a few years back talk about Syrian refugees coming by boat, I spoke up to a co-worker friend: "But I'm a boat refugee too." Their response was: "You're OK, you're the good kind," ' she explains. Passports are a class system, and one that can be weaponised for or against you, and this policing at borders is a type of violence. I wrote earlier about my difficulties at borders, despite the right visa or passport. But the reason I was able to challenge the border control officers was because I do know I am a 'good' immigrant. My New Zealand passport, my Australian birthplace, my adjacency to whiteness, my overeducation gave me a confidence to push back against challenging questioning.

Georgina explained her relationship with class. Her route into journalism was through the Scott Trust Bursary, which is a Guardian Foundation scheme designed to 'assist students who face financial difficulty in attaining qualifications'. The scheme supports a MA in journalism in selected universities, and offers work with the *Guardian*.

'My "working class" background has shaped, and in some ways become a limiting factor in my career more than my race, although the two are inextricably linked,' she says. Georgina is state-school educated and the first in her generation to go to university. Her parents worked nightshifts and two jobs each to survive. Her dad never attended school because he began working when he was eight years old. 'More often in the media industry, the discussion of diversity is about race and ethnicity, but [as] my mum often says "when you have money, you have confidence." '

Georgina points out to me that in a world that seems to reward those who 'have strong, bold ideas' and the ability to act with conviction and authority, class plays a huge factor. 'Growing up with little money, I wanted to make myself as small as possible – now, midway through my twenties, I am having to train myself to do the opposite, to stand taller and take up space. That is a huge challenge that I am still trying to navigate!' The intersection of class and race is complex, but it is about exclusion. Where are the spaces you're allowed and where are you not? Finding yourself suddenly in a place that makes you feel not just unwelcome but is very much *not for you* can be brutal; creating a physical reaction, a desire to be small.

Madévi Emmanuelle Dailly, a French Cambodian* travel and food writer based in Hastings, said to me, 'in the UK, I've found that class often trumps race. I can sound quite posh – I was, for a while, privately educated in Hong Kong – so when someone questions where I'm "originally" from, I just go full RP [Received Pronunciation]. That usually puts an end to their questioning. It's crass, but it will never cease to amuse me.'

This idea of exclusion and where the intersection of class and race comes into play, for me, is with tokenism. To be tokenised is a microaggression where you feel the weight of representation and also of not being valued. You are forced into a performative role. In many situations,

---

* When I asked Madévi about the specificities of her heritage she said: 'the easy answer is French Cambodian. But my father is also half American, his mother was half Black, and we allegedly have some Native American ancestors too. In short: who knows!'

I've found whiteness and middle class-ness as identities are allowed to be seen as expert, business-worthy/savvy, and ultimately a type of translator between culture. My presence has felt like a tickbox.

I have been asked to do many talks, to host panels and to participate in discussions, to give expert opinions. Often, I am offering an 'alternative' voice. Sometimes I don't mind being a 'diversity hire' because I have faith in my knowledge and my expertise. But almost every time I run into issues, where my time feels undervalued – the less I am paid, the more complicated the issues often are. Most of the time, I am happy to just point out a few things that would make the experience better for all. My friend Emma – who is white British and Oxbridge-educated, and who has experience in many spaces – has taken it upon herself to be email draft-er for times when things are uncomfortable for me. She is a) an excellent writer and b) separate from the situation, so is always able to succinctly put things where I would either over-explain, or overly apologise. She has also pointed out that trying to teach people how their (possibly unconscious) bias is affecting me and others is emotional labour. This is what an ally looks like.

Once, I was invited to a conference to host a panel of BIPOC American women to discuss shifting the white, male-dominated lens on food and food sovereignty that is prominent in US (and other) media landscapes, and to interview an author about her book which explored race and colonialism. I was told upfront that this wouldn't be paid, but I could have a ticket to the conference for free. I said yes immediately – the women sounded amazing, I was flattered. And lastly, I wanted to see the other talks.

But as time went on, a few things cropped up. I was put in a position of having to explain that they had scheduled the talk too early, and I couldn't afford to stay the night where the talks were being held, which was deeply embarrassing. The prep work was a lot: coordinating time differences for pre-panel Zoom meetings, buying (out of my own pocket) and reading the book, researching four people in-depth – all on top of a nosedive in freelance work, the rise in the cost of living, and the financial pressures of Christmas and the festive season.

At the last minute, I discovered (by looking at the schedule, rather than being told by the organisers) that both talks were ninety minutes long. This is a long time to be asking women to talk about their racialised identities, oppression and their efforts in trying to change the narratives. With a very early start to my day, I got to the city at 10.20 a.m. for the 11 a.m. talk. I wasn't given any instructions on how to find the venue and the conference website didn't have an address, just the name of the building. I walked around the block trying to find the entrance, and finally found a reception. The conference was in a diverse city but, walking through the hallowed buildings and open spaces of the famed institution the talk was held in, I didn't see one person of colour. At that point, I was flustered and lost. When I eventually found the building, I then had to walk into rooms to ask where I was supposed to be. Upon arrival, I realised there was a big main door, with conference volunteers around. How easy would it have been to put the details of the entrance on the website, or even on an email? Spaces like that are deeply unfamiliar to me. The experience was intimidating and unsettling. Just making access to a building easy (idiot-fluster-early-morning proof!) is a way to make someone feel welcome.

The first talk was poorly attended with approximately fifteen people. The issue here is that when you want to showcase diverse voices, it simply isn't enough to just give them a platform. You need to work hard to make sure those voices from the margins are heard. To paraphrase bell hooks – you need to work to make the 'margin the centre', otherwise it is just lip service and nothing changes.

After the first talk, my brain was full of wonderful information, and exhausted. I scurried away to a coffee shop to sit in silence. Before I knew it, a further ninety minutes had passed and I was stuffing a M&S sandwich down, before going on stage for talk number two. After that truly wonderful discussion, I was too tired to go and find any of the last talks of the day, and took myself back to London. Therefore, the fee – a ticket to the conference – was moot. I sat on the train, drained, feeling like this exchange had been exploitive, a colonial power dynamic. This day seems a small thing, but the experience is what I would describe as a microaggression.

These spaces of knowledge are white. The conferences, the 'renowned' person, the buildings built not so long ago off the money from plantations in stolen lands.* Even if it is not exclusively filled with white people, a white space is where white people can walk through without being questioned or feel the need to justify why they are there. For a person of colour to feel comfortable, you've had to have had access to such spaces and be familiar with them. The class system in the UK is complex. Just as how having a 'good' passport is a system of class, knowing these spaces and having the confidence to traverse them – having the money to stay the night and do an early morning talk – is a classed space that a lot of ESEA people don't have access to. My education gives me cultural capital that makes me feel comfortable in many places. Once I am in the room, and doing my job in front of people, I feel comfortable. But I didn't go to a fancy university. My childhood in New Zealand was a classic, state school, suburban single-parent family upbringing. There are many aspects of institutional spaces that I feel uncomfortable and unwelcome in.

To commission and curate with empathy and care is to be able to a look at the intersection of race and class, which will allow for organisations to make these places feel accessible. Tokenism is when that hasn't been interrogated. It may seem a stretch to say that classism and tokenism

---

* It was only in 2015 that British taxpayers 'paid off' debt the government agreed to in 1835 to compensate slave owners due to the abolition of slavery – therefore this is actually contemporary history; these places are spaces of violence, even if the buildings feel 'old' and were built generations ago.

is a topic for the chapter on violence, and I don't want to overstate a situation, but what it does is continue to perpetuate a sense of otherness and hostility, which is a microaggression in action. If you are continually finding yourself in these situations, it is exhausting to navigate. Dr Rasha Diab and Dr Beth Godbee write 'microaggressions are anything but small: Instead, as a form of violence, they have far-reaching consequences. Just as systemic injustice enables microaggressions, microaggressions perpetuate systemic injustice. In other words, the micro and macro are intricately related and reinforcing.'*[25]

I want to build new spaces away from these exclusive, tokenistic ones, but I also I think it is important for us to be in them. At the moment, they have power, and access to power is access to change. As a woman of colour, I was able to chair the talks sensitively for the other women of colour on stage, and my knowledge on colonialism, my expertise of editing and writing on food and farming made me appropriate. But I – we – can't be in those places if we are a token, made to feel undervalued or not worth listening to, but look good for the programme line-up.

There is a difference between diversity, inclusion and safe spaces. A diverse space has a lot of different people in a room. An inclusive space invites those people to speak. But a safe space is where those 'diverse' people feel comfortable to speak without invitation, without being

---

*   This article looks at studies in microaggression, and determining the relationship with macro and micro.

questioned on their existence, and where they will not only be heard but they know they will be listened to and will be understood.

I just want us to be safe.

Chapter 4

Gender

I became acutely aware about my racialised place in the world at the same time as I was beginning to understand desire, sexuality and my body. My gender, and how it intersected with race, was my crucial and brutal introduction to realising exactly how my difference played out in public. My identity was not my own but seemed to belong to the world at large. It was for others to decide who I was.

Those awkward teenage years were where I experimented with make up (too much of it, poorly applied), or wearing boys' T-shirts, loose-fitting to cover any curves, outfits bought at the army surplus store. I ricocheted between wanting to explore my personal identity and gender, and wanting to hide from the world and the predatory looks I was receiving. At eighteen, I didn't just feel the looks, but I heard the words that put my body on a stage for others. Everyone is beautiful at eighteen. Then, like now, my hair was long. I'd discovered hair straightening products, and I was desperate to tame my hair, make it obedient. I had just stopped dancing and playing sports so everything about my body was slowly softening. I weighed

50 kilograms, had a C-cup bra size, and strange men in the street would tell me I had 'big tits for an Asian'. A renowned amateur theatre director told me if I wanted to study theatre in London, I should audition for the 'proper schools' because: 'I was just the right type of exotic they'd want.' What she meant was I was different enough to be interesting, but familiar enough to be desirable, non-threatening, not dangerous. The 'right' things were my whiteness, my thinness, my youth, my long hair. I felt like she was describing a product for sale. It was 2000 and for a moment in time, I was perfect – for a very specific lens. To be told that your flavour of difference is OK in other people's mouths is bitter. I was navigating racialised gender and sexuality at a time when celebrity magazines were ripping apart women like it was war or sport.

I have a joke about how white men flirt with me, trying to guess where I am from, without me uttering a word. Then I speak with the broadest New Zealand accent I can muster, and their disappointment is palpable. They want something far flung, 'exotic'. The most common guess in a dimmed bar is South America – Chile or Peru, usually – from white men who have been to South America for three to six months (any shorter they know it's a holiday, any longer they know they don't know anything). These men have insisted that I must know Spanish even after I've said 'No, I said I'm half Malaysian!' I am but a blank exotic canvas for fantasies to be projected on.

I remember being a child at ballet, and the mothers discussing making sure outfits were adjustable so that when we grew they didn't have to make or buy a new character skirt and the like. One of the mothers nodded to me, and said to my mother: 'Well, yes, your girls mature faster than ours, don't they?' with a slight hand gesture demonstrating curves. I remember thinking, *what was my body going to do that my white friends' bodies wouldn't?* The sexualisation of my body was seen at the age of eight.

When you are othered, you are hyper-aware of how much space your body takes up. The racism in school was contained to microaggressions that I could brush off, but entering into the adult world, for me, felt dangerous. I had internalised so much about the ways I could be acceptable, palatable, that I was constantly aware of when my body was misbehaving. My hair was frizzy, my skin marked by freckles, spots, moles. My body was rounded and my thighs were built for running through jungles, whereas Asian women were (I thought! Media told me!) supposed to be small and delicate.

I have spent so long trying to tame myself, trying to choose an acceptable racial identity or an ambiguity or to lean into my whiteness. Every day, I still think about how I can move through space, how I will meet with people and I ask myself: *How will they see me? What do I want them to see?*

In a world now of video calls, my face becomes a site of uncomfortableness and is fraught with (self) hatred. I spent a week on Zoom calls with white people. During one interview, with a really lovely and interesting white woman, I became aware of our physical differences.

The width of my nose, the slant of my eyes, the pallor of my skin mid-winter when it really needs to see the sun – everything felt in contrast to her, and my internal systems interpreted that as negative. Vera and I were on a podcast once, and we spoke about these moments where you stop and realise 'shit, I'm not white!' These moments are jolting. In a very visceral way, you realise you are not 'the norm' in a white world, and that is understood as A Bad Thing. It is often gendered as well as racialised. That Zoom call was yet another moment of self-realisation – of being ugly, of being unacceptable, of 'shit, I'm not white!'

I only realised how much that Zoom call affected me two days later, after I had back-to-back Zoom calls with people for this book. An abundance of Asian faces! I was positively bouncing off walls with enthusiasm for life. I stopped and thought about the week and the way I had felt. Seeing myself reflected (albeit online) was incredibly important. It normalised me; I didn't have to think about my body, my face in the spaces I was occupying. I was able to simply exist.

Nicole Ocran, co-author of the 2024 book *The Half of It* and co-host of *Mixed Up* podcast, is a content creator in the fashion industry. For Nicole, who is Ghanaian and Filipino, there is the added complexity of being read as Black 'as default'. She explained how once a cab driver commented that she had got 'absolutely nothing from your [Filipino] mom'. This is something that used to hurt a lot more, but she has been able to navigate it because she understands that her Asian-ness is something that can't be taken away from her. She explains there is an assumption that being mixed is being Black and white as the census tick boxes options iterate, particularly in the UK (Nicole is originally from the US). Therefore, for here, it is important to articulate that she is not white. 'There are nuances in being Asian.'

Being in the public eye and within the world of fashion means she feels she has to articulate her heritage often, and the intersection of race and gender comes up a lot. 'There is an otherness, but that is also in contrast with people looking to you to be a solution to their own problems about race and gender. There's a lot of additional emotional labour that's not necessarily within your control. This looks like questions, this looks like unsolicited advice or unsolicited traumatic content in your DMs, and this looks like white people believing that you owe them something because they follow you so they tend to demand things of you.'

Nicole explains that this difference means there are conversations, frustrations, ethics and moral obligations that are important to her to be vocal about. 'Working as a fashion influencer who is a mixed Black and Asian woman, I'm just operating in these spaces and online in a completely different way to my white peers and colleagues.' There is a running thread with the people I have spoken with, this idea of responsibility, and the need (and want) to speak up. It is a deep urge to want to see change.

I don't want to hide my ethnicity and heritage and I don't want to play up to it. I still chemically straighten my hair and curse my thighs, but I am finding my way into being the wrong kind of exotic – dangerous and uncomfortable, speaking out. My friend Frankie and I talk about identity a lot (she is mixed race too, white British and Dominican heritage). She said to me once: 'We are doing the work so that our great-great grandchildren will be OK, safe and do not have to do this work.' I think about this all the time, the unlearning in ourselves, so that each generation passes on less embodied emotions of otherness. It is a lifetime's work, navigating our own identity and intersections.

Catriona James, an actor, mover and performance maker based in Cardiff, told me that their journey through race has also had parallels with their gender journey. We discuss the idea of becoming aware and a 'dawning' of ideas around gender and race. Catriona, whose mother is Chinese Malaysian and father is British Canadian, explains to me 'I grew up thinking of myself as white – I mean, I look pretty white, right? – until the world told me in a thousand painful ways that I wasn't.' Catriona also thought that if they were a woman, then everything they did should be 'feminine' by default, except they felt 'alien' when in groups of, particularly cis-het, women. 'The many unhelpful stereotypes of what "Asian girls" should look like have always sharpened my experience of what I now recognise as a degree of gender dysphoria. I do not physically match that picture of petite, slim, hairless – where it counts – femininity,' Catriona expands. 'There's things I can laugh at now, but they used to be so painful: the classic aunty comments on my weight every time I was back in Malaysia; being called butch by aunties back in my early twenties when I had a shaved head.'

Catriona also explains the conscious decision to embrace their Chinese-ness, which is part of not seeing themselves as 'half'. 'I am Chinese. I am also white.' Therefore, they are trying to focus on ways in which they are Chinese, such as learning Mandarin, teaching themselves how to cook mainland Chinese dishes. Looking at traditional Chinese clothing, Catriona points out how the intersection of race and gender can play out. The form-fitting cheongsam was too 'hyper-feminine' for them to feel comfortable in. 'I really want a loose sam foo, like what my poh poh [grandmother] always used to wear – a top with the classic Chinese collar and loose trousers or culottes. It's actually quite a unisex outfit, cut similarly for men and women.' Catriona spent six months in China in 2018, which was a key point in navigating their racialised identity. 'I was roughly in the part of China that my mum's grandfathers came from when they immigrated to Malaya. My Chinese-ness has always been othering in my life, but in China it meant commonality. That was huge. With regards to gender as well, it was healing to spend time surrounded by a broader spectrum of specifically Chinese femininity. Of course, open queerness is not super safe in mainland China or even Hong Kong, but I clocked queer women and queer folk. And even outside of queerness, I saw working-class Chinese women everywhere, with their earthiness and obvious strength. It was healing to realise that that is where I come from too.'

Looking back to our heritages, and beyond the whiteness norms that we live in here, is a way to reconfigure our identity that includes how we see gender. There is a beautiful reflection in June Bellebono's essay 'Ladyboy' in *East Side Voices*, where as a child she looked to her Burmese uncles. In them, she saw the difference of masculinity presented in South East Asia: 'I had always been read as feminine, regardless of my sexuality or gender identity – and I believe that's also due to growing up as an Asian boy in a white environment. Timidity, cuteness, innocence and sensitivity were some of the qualities that were attributed to me, and often contributed to the emasculated idea of Asian men. Reflecting on it now, I value these qualities. I value the fact that, in my experience, my Burmese uncles would often embrace softness and intimacy.'[1]

Looking to the stories of my childhood has been a way for me to look beyond ideas of binaries or the constructed norms I grew up with in New Zealand and then the UK. The first part of my childhood in Sarawak was filled with stories, in particular told to me by my inek (grandmother), with my favourite being the comedic tales of Apai Saloi. Within these stories, much like many folk tales, existed a world that was intertwined with gods and spirits. My inek was a huge believer in the supernatural world. She once (when I was an adult!) wouldn't stay with me alone as she believed I wasn't strong enough to scare off the ghosts – she made my much younger cousin stay the night too.

I don't know when I first started understanding a binary gender divide, or when I rejected the idea of it and challenged the idea of a binary lens on other aspects in my life. But I do know that, although I use she/her pronouns and am cis-het, the idea of multiple gender identities seems incredibly normal to me. I believe those early Iban stories set up a world for me outside the colonial and capitalist structures that enforce binaries. When you look at a world that is based on nature, that looks closely at the environment and landscape, it is impossible to find hard binaries and linear systems. Within Iban culture there has always been what anthropologists have referred to as the 'third gender', and I have known women within Iban communities who now might identify with being trans or gender non-conforming. These 'third gender' people hold a particularly sacred space within Iban folklore. Traditionally they were the highest level of 'shaman',* referred to as manang bali, and in Gawai origin stories were charged with taking gifts to the gods to invite them to the Gawai feast. I remember these women sitting on

---

* It's believed that the last of this level of shaman died in the late 1800s, but these non-gender conforming or trans shaman continue to feature in folklore.[2]

the floor in the kitchen pounding the tapioca leaves for dinner, the place where all the aunties would be.

I would like to note that the term 'third gender' is one that is used mostly in reference to non-white cultures, particularly Indigenous communities, and I find it a problematic term. It still alludes to a linear concept of identity or hard definitions and sense of binary, whereas there are more fluidity, spectrums and grey areas to be understood. And it seems to be a white, Western, academic label placed on non-white bodies. I hope that we can find language that better encapsulates non-binary ideas. American cartoonist Alison Bechdel – who conceived the Bechdel Test, a quick feminist litmus test for films – was interviewed for the *Guardian* in 2023 and spoke about the Western perceptions of queerness and ability for change. 'If humanity even survives another 100 years, which I'm not so sure of, I think that there's going to be a lot less attachment to sexual or even gender identity. I think it's going to be much more fluid and we'll be fine with it.'[3] It is this move away from a Western concept of gender, to be more fluid, that I think will help untangle a lot of how we look at race, and identity as a whole.

It seems funny to say, but looking into the Iban farming systems for my PhD is what made me rethink my relationship with gender and race. The Iban are a farming society and are structurally fairly equalitarian (at least traditionally they are) with regards to class and gender. There are gender divides particularly in tasks around war, for example: no one can go to war unless a blanket has been woven, a task women do – therefore making weaving women's 'war'. Everyone farms, drinks, dances, dreams of gods and good omens, and can be a community leader. It feels a practical society. I get to see my gender – alongside other genders – as having a place to belong and be part of a community, not as a commodity. In June's essay, she writes about how researching queer and trans identities in South East Asia 'showed me a new understanding of what my body and identity could look and feel like, outside of Western paradigms. Exposure, knowledge and self-reflection helped connect the dots. Things in my life stared to make sense.'4

I write this knowing that I do have a nostalgic lens on Iban culture as I have done my growing up mostly in the West and so can miss the complexities of the everyday-ness of a culture. But I also know that part of the colonial project was to bring a Christian god to native peoples, to instil a commodities-based economy and drum out any blurred edges, fluidity and a multiplicity of Indigenous beliefs. I can't begin to imagine what our world would be like if European powers hadn't tried to eradicate those ways of living from us; it could've been beautiful. This isn't to say that all/any ESEA cultures are utopias of equality and fluid gender identities and expressions – far from it. But looking into our own heritages and the various nuances of our different cultures can help us find ways to exist and be ourselves, and be comfortable in ourselves.

I often joke that I blame the Victorians for everything. It is true that the accelerated growth of industry and expanding wealth from (and power over) the colonies along with the establishment of 'the middle class', coupled with strict codes of morality and ideas of family structure, erased cultural nuances (or at least tried very hard to) through rules and regulations. With rapid growth of towns and cities, bureaucracy thrived and new laws were imposed, such as the Labouchere Amendment in 1885 in Britain, making male homosexuality ('gross indecency') illegal for the first time and subject to policing by growing police forces. Academic and therapist Meg-John Barker and illustrator Jules Scheele outline in their book, *Gender: A Graphic Guide*, how the increased gender division in the West grew due to the industrial revolution and the growth of 'trade-based capitalism', entwining class and gender, and the ideal family structure. Women stayed at home doing unpaid work, and men did paid labour that was seen as more valuable. They also explain how patriarchal structures work with other systems of oppression such as 'capitalism, colonialism, white supremacy . . . so we can never tease gender apart from other categories like class, race, sexuality or disability.'[5]

Safiah, my London-based Malaysian-born friend, tells me that in the playground she is often mistaken as the nanny of her son. The intersection of gender and race of a feminised brown body is automatically associated with care and labour. 'There was an incident where we were playing in the communal gardens near us. Along with a nanny looking after the neighbour's baby, we were chatting and she was asking, "What's the boy's [her son, Skyler] heritage?" And I said, "My husband's from Hereford." I had to say a few times: "My husband's from Hereford. So [my son is] half English," before it clicked to her that I'm not his nanny and that Skyler is my baby. This made me think "Oh, maybe that's why at swimming, only the nannies speak to me, and the mums aren't really friendly." Those moments remind me that I'm brown, I'm a foreigner and an immigrant.'

In Safiah's story, where a racialised body represents an other within a feminised space, I am reminded about how 'sisterhood' is often a fallacy. Feminism can only exist and work when it is intersectional and interrogates these meetings of identities. Academic Chandra Talpade Mohanty explains that placing 'women' as a category produces an idea of 'sameness'. When a universal approach like that is taken, we see norms being constructed. The norm is always a middle-class culture which 'codifies peasant and working-class histories and cultures as Other,' Mohanty writes.[6] When race comes into play, then the norm is positioned as white as well. Therefore, in a global north and Western space of the UK, we have to investigate and look at gender through multiple intersections – class, colonialism, race.

I have written that looking back at histories and discovering stories from our past, our cultures and our childhoods can help find a sense of belonging. But the act of telling our own stories, like June has done, and telling new stories helps us find a future for us to belong in.

Resy* international editor David reminds me that I have written three pieces on gender in the restaurant industry for Resy – on systems of patriarchy, safety in hospitality and ESEA women in the industry. For David, it isn't enough to just tell these stories; it is key to have the right people interviewed and the right people writing them. 'Early on, I tried to make it a point to commission writers who were women or people of colour to write about other women or people of colour in order to share unfiltered perspectives, and the kind of expertise and authority that can only originate from those with lived experience. It shapes everything – the questioning, the rapport between interviewer and the person being interviewed.' He explains that the majority of British media is still dominated by 'whiteness and cis male perspectives'. As one of the few restaurant editors who is a person of colour, he feels a responsibility to represent a segment of the industry that might not often be talked about 'in their own terms'. Mohanty's points about sameness are made to address a need and a way to find solidarity. It is through considered actions for voices to be heard 'in their own terms', as David says, that allows for a sense of collectiveness that brings in diverse intersections.

---

* Resy London stopped in early 2024, globally the company still exists.

*

Gender is a social construct honed by capitalism and colonialism, and shaped by our Western understanding of race, class, ableism and many other intersections of identities.* The cis-het family unit is a productive structure for our consumer-based world, which is very much structured around gender norms. Within diasporic families, diving into family dynamics, passing down heritage, knowledge sharing across generations and exploring legacy feel like ways to disrupt and shift ideas around gender. Finding ways of belonging in a world that others, and teaching the next generations about belonging within familial ties, can create wider community. Discovering the extended boundaries of what is family, what is chosen family, in our chosen home of the UK is queering the norms, is taking agency and is living outside of binaries. It is impossible to talk about gender without thinking about other intersections, and I think it is impossible to think about family and community without seeing the connection with gender.

It wasn't until Catriona was forty-three that they started using gender neutral pronouns, but it wasn't a clear-cut decision either. 'I prefer "they", but I hang on to "she" because the political category of woman is deeply important to me. But I find a lot of freedom in considering myself

---

* Judith Butler, and in particular their book *Gender Trouble: Feminism and the Subversion of Identity*, is a good place to start to investigate this topic.

non-binary.' Catriona tells me that in many ways, race and gender are a painful intersection, but it has made them who they are. 'I wouldn't have it any other way. I saw something on Instagram: "queerness is a long thread of hurt – what will you mend with that thread?"* That's how we navigate it, isn't it? Mend what we can, with what we've been given.' For Catriona, their close-knit queer community in Cardiff has been a huge part of the mending; Catriona is building their own family, on their own terms. In diaspora, the building of family is crucial in creating home and belonging.

Within the more traditional family structure, the ritual of homemaking is often the responsibility of diasporic migrant women. It is often not seen as creative or of value. Feminist academic Irene Gedalof† writes that in the context of migration, performing the 'same' rituals of making home, such as cooking or cleaning, can take on new meanings. At each iteration of these seemingly repetitive tasks, creativity is happening, home is being built and

---

* An Instagram post by @queer_death_stories of a tweet by @sagescrittore: 'last night Ursula K. Le Guin visited my dreams and I said to her "Queerness is a long thread of hurt" and she answered "Now what will you mend with that thread?" and it rocked me so hard I woke up crying'.[7]
† In her journal article 'Birth, Belonging and Migrant Mothers', feminist academic Irene Gedalof explains the feminised work in building belonging in new spaces – Gedalof was my PhD supervisor and her work was key in my own research of South East Asian identity and migration.

created as familiarity seeds itself into the everyday.[8] The smell of rice cooking coats the space and reminds you that this is home, objects anchor a place and allows you to feel like it's yours. These actions are often thought of as feminised, but recognising the strength and power in these actions shifts the value of those who perform them, and allows us to investigate who else performs these rituals. The building of home is done in a multiplicity of ways.

Artist Youngsook Choi explains to me that as a mother, she doesn't feel the need to 'carry the gendered burden for holding and inheriting my culture'. She does often initiate the Korean and Jewish (her son's father's heritage) celebrations because 'I operate these celebrations as a way of building affectionate communities around us. As a migrant nuclear family, I always feel the necessity to build an alternative extended family, which is a very difficult mission in London, such a transient city.'

For Helena Lee, an author and editor whose heritage is Chinese Malaysian, instilling a connection with her and her husband's heritage in her daughters was an important and deliberate aspect of parenting. 'Before they [their daughters] were born, my partner – who is white British – and I spoke about it a lot, and it was really important that the responsibility lay with both of us, not just on me.' Food has been an important way into this creation of legacy. 'The very act of gung gung [Helena's father] making dumplings with them in the way that his mother did with him is evidence of that cultural transference.' But storytelling has been and is crucial to Helena.

'Cultural heritage is made up of individual stories, and I do believe every story counts.' It is with this in mind that *East Side Voices*, the book and an event series, was created. Helena thought very literally about the generations after us – expanding a sense of a parental passing on of story to a wide, non-familial audience – and 'the cultural landscape they were entering into, it seemed absolutely appalling that it was a place that was potentially hostile, and undermined their sense of belonging. *East Side Voices* was an attempt to change the way the world saw us, as well as a way to change the way we saw ourselves.'

A matriarchal network has been a huge source of support and grounding in identity for Nicole Ocran. She grew up close to her mother and her titas (aunts), both literal aunts and those women in the extended family-like network. Being Filipino was never something she questioned. Early memories are of family: Sundays after church, birthdays, holidays, cooking and food. The kitchen has always been a place to gather. Food is not only a huge part of the Filipino culture but is also a comfort, a source of love for her. When Nicole is sick, her mother cooks arroz caldo, and each time she goes home her mother teaches her something different. Cooking is also an act of remembering, a legacy to pass on to generations. 'My Tita Chel, who is the eldest of my mom's sisters, passed away about three years ago, and my cousin and I copied her recipe book to make sure it didn't get lost.' Thinking about the future is where questions about language come up for Nicole. She understands bits and pieces of Tagalog but doesn't know how to speak it. 'I want to have children someday and would love for them to know the language. I know it's not really something I can control, but keeping those connections is really important to me. I still feel pangs of guilt around not knowing it and have been looking up Tagalog classes.'

Youngsook thinks about the connection between generations with a fluid approach. The 'natural weaving of complex cultural identity mostly comes from joy practice in the celebration of Lunar New Year and other seasonal Korean folk traditions and rich food culture around them,' she tells me. 'I don't want him [her son] to be either Korean or Jewish. I want him to explore the liminal terrain where he can constantly shift in between and question the very idea of cultural and national identities. The marginal space out of the marginalised. I want him to find and build his own community beyond this territorial sense of belonging.'

When I asked KS Tong, a London-based accountant, about learning about identity and passing these learnings on, we spoke about the question 'where are you from?' He answers the question with 'New Zealand, but my heritage is from Hong Kong,' and feels that the combativeness and divisiveness of the question disappears then. 'But I think I have also been moulded by my mother who was very aware that she was living in a foreign country, in New Zealand, and we had to respect local customs. So to that point, there was no competition or complementing per se but dare I say, there was quiet submissiveness? You can explore this in different ways. Was she compromising herself? Or was she just being respectful? Whatever it was, the result is that I feel that my culture and heritage can be worked into a Western lifestyle as opposed to combating it.' He is also very conscious of passing on a sense of identity to his mixed (Chinese and European) children, which is imparting this continued journey of from-ness. 'I talk to my kids every day in Chinese. I feel a responsibility to pass on our heritage and culture to them. I have actually found this quite difficult and humbling because I realise the gaps in my own knowledge are so large. But it has never made me prouder to be Asian to be honest.'

Editor David Paw echoes KS's feelings about gaps in knowledge. Becoming a new father created a sense of urgency to 'find himself' – 'as the stakes now involve failing my son by not teaching him about his Karen heritage; failing my ancestors as a cultural dead end of presumably centuries of good decision-making; and failing myself for all of the above.' With the ongoing military rule after the 2021 coup in Myanmar, not being able to connect physically with the culture adds another set of borders. David feels lucky as his wife is also of diaspora – Indian heritage, raised in Canada – and they rarely have to explain themselves and cultural subtleties such as 'deference, the collective vs the individual, taking your fucking shoes off when you enter the house – yet there's enough difference to appreciate the positives about each other's culture.'

Discussing parental responsibilities of passing on heritage brings up questions of masculinity for David. Finding ways to understand his Asian-ness is also about understanding gender. 'Growing up in the north of England, it's difficult to find cues of how to exist as a person of colour, but especially as a person of East or South East Asian heritage,' David says. Part of gaining an understanding and relationship with his identity was understanding others' assumptions about him, which included a combination of viewing Asian men through the lens of twentieth-century popular culture and a flattening of Asian-ness, and that 'I do not fit most people's expectations of Asian male tropes'. David tells me that as a straight, able-bodied man, he's very aware of the privilege he has within both his community but also in society in general. David feels that the racism and aggression he may experience under white supremacy and patriarchy may not always be considered worthy of in-depth dialogue, which can occasionally feel sobering. But at the same time, he says, it is always important to acknowledge 'being born in a society that still favours maleness, and that within Asian communities, we're still in possession of the most privilege by some margin'. David says that he's dissected the intersection of race and masculinity over and over again, but what he keeps coming back to is being able to focus on what he can control, to hopefully lead by example, 'to try and be someone that a younger version of me would have looked up to'.

Frit Tam, a multi-hyphen creative who has won awards

for his adventure documentary filmmaking, is based in Sheffield and is second-generation British-born Chinese. He explains to me that 'as a trans guy, I have a really interesting relationship with gender, and in terms of my ethnicity, I feel like I have a huge respect for my culture and my heritage but I have a very "Western" way of looking at things.' This can sometimes feel like a clash – where at times his views on his heritage, based on his upbringing, can feel a bit more conservative. In contrast, 'I tend to live my life as a trans person in a very out and proud way. Sometimes this feels as if there's a bit of a dichotomy going on that I have to navigate between my nationality and my cultural heritage and the way that I live my life.' Frit does caution that although he currently feels lucky to be in a country where he can be 'out and proud', this might not be easy or possible in years to come due to the overt oppression of trans people in the UK.

Most of Frit's family are in Hong Kong, so it is a small unit that is in the UK. They are close because he feels they are all they have, which is precious: 'I get the sense that we sort of hold tight onto each other.' Frit explains that they find ways to resolve any frictions or tensions that may arise, and despite being dotted all over the country, they make the effort to meet up. He speaks to me about telling his parents he was trans and how he prefers to frame it as 'letting in' as opposed to 'coming out'. 'The first time I let my parents in was when I came out about my sexuality. And then the second time I let them in, was about my gender. Both times it was difficult. I was nervous, I was worried about it. I didn't know necessarily what they were going to say. But they've fortunately been brilliant. And what I've really learnt from the past couple of years since I let them in, was that it's really important to take the process at a comfortable pace and with transparency, so that my parents felt included, particularly at big milestones.' Frit explains that the process rattled everything he understood about himself and society, but it was important to find a way to go through the journey together with his parents.

David told me that when speaking with other men in the ESEA community, he found that very few are aware of their intersection of race and gender, and therefore are often not open to dialogue with others about it. This lack of recognition – both in themselves but also in popular storytelling – means that ESEA men may not see themselves as part of a collective, but rather as individuals. This affects the notion of belonging and building community, with each other but also with the wider ESEA community.

'Some of the most prominent Asian male figures in popular [Western] culture in the past century have been hugely unflattering portrayals of Asian masculinity – or lack thereof – that have subconsciously shaped the treatment of generations upon generations of Asian men in the same way that a single scene in *Full Metal Jacket* has been hugely damaging for generations of Asian women,' David tells me. He has a list: 'Mickey Rooney in yellowface in *Breakfast at Tiffany's*; Long Duk Dong in *Sixteen Candles*;

Han in *Two Broke Girls*; literally anything Ken Jeong is in; every emotionless Asian henchman, infantilised Asian sidekick or romantically uninterested martial arts expert with a perfect physique that's made their way onto Western screens in the past century... Each of them has shaped society's perception of Asian men, and as an Asian man, it can be difficult not to internalise some of that, too.'

Most of these specific examples are American, and when you look at the people that are shifting the narrative, they are also American ('Steven Yeun, Manny Jacinto, Ali Wong, Paul Feig and surprisingly white women – though I suspect the latter is an attempted public riposte to white toxic masculinity as opposed to a genuine desire to present Asian men in a better light,' David points out). We are in dire need of our own stories, of stories in our own space. Belonging is about recognising ourselves and our lives in the narratives we see in the world, and I will discuss problematic depictions of ESEA people – particularly women – in the next chapter.

When I asked Frit about negative portrayals of gender in relation to race, he changed my framing of the question and said that ultimately we are all looking to belong. 'I just deeply believe that anything that impacts our sense of belonging is a negative. We should always be pursuing behaviours and conversations that enhance belonging instead.' He expands, 'LGBTQIA+ people have obviously experienced a huge sense of being othered.' This needs to change. In Jake Hall's 2024 book, *Shoulder to Shoulder: A Queer History of Solidarity, Coalition and Chaos*, they write in-depth about the solidarity between racialised communities and queer communities – not in the least because there are queer people of colour. The book points out that this idea of enhancing belonging must be seen as a coalition between marginalised identities. We intersect and connect in many different ways and can thread our lives together to build strength and community.[9]

In 2021, Frit went on a 1,700-kilometre trip by bike and rollerblades from Newcastle to Brighton called Glide for Pride, interviewing people within the LGBTQIA+ community up and down the country. Frit filmed the trip – all seventy-one days – and is raising money to turn it into a film. Frit explains in the trailer that it is an adventure film, with LGBTQIA+ people at the forefront. It is shot beautifully, weaving the landscape of England and individuals, in their homes, in public spaces – and it captures a sense of not just a community but a country based on collectiveness. This project started off as a research mission and became a way to find and demonstrate belonging.

But what is important alongside building community is the work of activism, which is to make sure that we are doing work that does address safety, does make change. As David explains in how and why he commissions: 'Aside from restaurants, my main interest is in experiences of Asian-ness in the diaspora so finding opportunities where the two intersect has always been something myself and colleagues [who are East Asian] are always interested in exploring, while doing our best to build in an overarching sense of responsibility to racial and social justice in our storytelling.'

Frit tells me, 'When I was presenting as a woman, I remember a friend asking me what part of my identity makes me feel least safe, the options were: being Chinese, being gay and being a woman. [Presenting as] a woman was what made feel unsafe.' Now the three options are: being Chinese, being queer and being a trans man, 'I think [now] being trans might be the least safe part of my identity because of all the anti-trans rhetoric going on at the moment.' Frit explains to me this is a complicated space to occupy in the UK because the majority of the hate is targeting trans women. 'It's very important that I stay strong as an ally for trans women, because they are ultimately the ones with the bullseye on their backs at the moment, trans women and drag queens. So as much as I have my own sort of individual perspectives on safety, ultimately, my priority more so is to try and stand up against trans misogyny.'

This is why Frit's work, such as Glide for Pride, feels so important, because it shows a collectiveness in the LGBTQIA+ community, and an allyship, but it also shows representation. His work tells all of us stories of diverse identities, so that marginalised people will not be seen as marginal but as belonging to a wider society. This is the work that changes the world. And there are so many stories being told, and looking to be told.

It is this sense of collectiveness and desire to support each other that I have seen demonstrated throughout the research for this book. There has always been racism, and there has always been community, but the experience of Covid-19 and its impact upon ESEA people has fostered a somewhat ferocious passion to connect and build, particularly in younger generations: millennials and Gen Z. A number of these groups look to inclusive gendered belonging; such as the ESEA Sisters who create physical spaces (hiking, marching, festivals and more) for ESEA women, trans, non-binary and genderqueer folk, and anchor their activity in ideas of resistance. In the next two chapters, I will talk more about the creative spaces of togetherness that I have been involved in that have counteracted otherness and un-belonging.

Chapter 5

Arts and Culture

We're all Scarlett Johansson.*

This joke is old and boring, but also it is forever funny. My friends and I still laugh about it years later. We have to – the idea that stories from East and South East Asia can be appropriated by Western media without consideration is part of the colonial dynamic that we still live with. The joke is funny but we are also still living it every day. We are here for consumption, every part of us: our food, our culture, our bodies. The story that Johansson was inadvertently caught up in in 2017 was about whitewashing ESEA stories; inspiration without examination of power. It is, of course, not Johansson's fault, not really; she is a stand-in for the many white artists who had the option to choose other non-problematic roles but didn't, or who are financially stable enough to turn down work but again, choose not to. She is not the only person to have seen this wholly inappropriate casting decision and either failed to recognise its inappropriateness, or failed

---

* Google 'Ghost in the Shell' and you will find all the context you need here.

to say anything about it. But the real issue at the heart of this joke is the lack of ESEA stories being told in global north spaces by ESEA people.

Storytelling is traditionally a way of explaining and passing on a culture and a set of belief systems to the next generation. It is a way to form identity, to create community and belonging. It is also a passing down of history and legacy, a way to remember and to reinforce culture. I often recall the Iban stories of my childhood that softly tell of multiple ways of looking at things, of banishing a binary and believing in the spirits in the trees. And I have told my own story in these pages. Storytelling for me is continuing a heritage, and also making a mark on the world, to say I am here. It is a way to bear witness and to record our existence. To tell our stories is to show we matter. The stories we tell are crucial to our society.

Whitewashing the original source of a story takes away the cultural context. Casting a white person as an ESEA character, or employing a white writer, producer or director to tell an ESEA story, means that the people whose culture that story is from are unable to see themselves and/or their heritage in a modern context. We are not able to see how we fit into the world we live in if our stories are not allowed to be told in a way that make sense to us, with *our* bodies telling *our* own stories.

Part of the 'Scarlett Johansson' conversation is about who can play what role. Because of the lack of parts for

ESEA actors, it is hurtful to see roles that are steeped in ESEA lore being played by white actors. Scarlett Johansson is far from the first actor to cosplay as an ESEA character. In the 2015 film *Aloha*, Emma Stone played Allison Ng, a character with Chinese heritage, and in 2016, the character of The Ancient One in *Doctor Strange*, originally a Tibetan man, was played by Tilda Swinton. Casting directors have seemingly learnt few lessons from those mistakes. In 2022, Brad Pitt and Joey King played Japanese characters in the film *Bullet Train*, and the adaptation of the book *Maria Beetle* by Kotaro Isaka relegated East Asian actors to the periphery even while being set in Japan. What does this say about how whiteness is valued, in opposition to Asian-ness? All of this raises an important question about representation. What do I mean by representation, and what is 'good' representation? Where can nuances be achieved?

In the 2018 film *Crazy Rich Asians*, British Malaysian actor Henry Golding's casting was pulled into question because of his mixed-race identity – his whiteness was raised as a key issue. A main criticism of Golding was that he wasn't Chinese, yet he was playing a character written as Chinese in the original book. Coupled with the fact he is half white, his casting was seen as Hollywood being reluctant to cast a 'full Chinese' or 'full Asian' person as a romantic lead. It was his adjacency to whiteness that had got him the role, critics said. Although I understand the idea of casting a non-Chinese actor as a Chinese character should be questioned, I also wonder how we define the correct 'face'? Golding is half white, half Iban. Does he have to wait until a story is written about his exact mix before he is allowed to be on screen? There were other problems with the film – Singapore is an incredibly racially diverse country, yet the film depicted only Chinese Singaporeans, ignoring the Malay and Indian populations. But there were many positives too. American actor and 2023 Oscar-winner Ke Huy Quan, of Vietnamese heritage and Chinese descent, cited the film as his inspiration for getting back into acting during the promotional tour for *Everything Everywhere All at Once*.[1] Does the commercial success of *Crazy Rich Asians* override the specifics of casting and cultural specificity, and create change and inspiration? Is seeing faces like, or similar to, yours the key in becoming recognised and valued? I think it's a start.

As well as Scarlett Johansson, I am also Henry Golding.

We're both half Iban and half (white) British – albeit I'm via New Zealand. He once posted a photo of his friend from London days, who was a bartender at Big Chill just off Brick Lane at the time I used to date another bartender there, and so I have a feeling Henry and I may have been at the same parties (Henry, did we hang out and not know!?). Which, if true, would be wild – two Ibans in one London venue!

It feels surreal but wonderful to have an Iban in mainstream popular culture, a recognition of a part of myself that is so hard to articulate. It's hard to believe people might now understand this side of me when I have spent my life trying to explain the idea of indigeneity, of Sarawak, of the name Iban as separate from 'headhunters of Borneo'. But, although Golding does talk about being Iban, within the wider conversation around him it seems to be a muted aspect of his identity. What I mean by this is that identity gets defined in binaries – e.g. not Asian enough, not white enough, a concept a lot of mixed-race people feel – and by doing that, the nuances of our identities and histories get forgotten or written out. Therefore, the narrative Golding has become wrapped up in is one of general 'Asian-ness' and his Sarawakian (Indigenous) heritage is often erased. Within discourse on 'being Asian', he is relegated to his whiteness. Yet within any Western space he will never be seen as white; in that lens he is 'Asian', he is 'other'. But an 'other' without the nuance of Iban-ness. When we tell our stories, we need to allow for this multiplicity, to not get caught up in 'enough-ness' or to diminish complex parts of our and others' identity.

In case you can't tell, I loved *Crazy Rich Asians*. I love romcoms as a genre. It is a storytelling structure that gets to exist both in fantasy and reality, the fairy-tale stories of childhood but with modern, relatable contexts. This is a genre where anything can happen, and often it does. It is a model that allows for, and has power to, subvert, suspend belief and play with established norms – we can see a possibility of diverse, non-binary realities, because deep down we all love to love. In the last few years there have been a spate of ESEA actors featuring in romcoms. I enjoyed the British actor George Young's performance as a vapid rich influencer in the Lindsay Lohan film *Falling for Christmas*. A favourite romcom of mine is *Last Christmas*, which stars Henry Golding as a kind, handsome person; there is an immigrant story in this film, but it's the lead character's Eastern European one. Both these characters aren't about race and so there is freedom in this representation, even though they are secondary characters, peripheral. Other Hollywood romcoms with mixed-race couples, such as *Love Hard* (2021), the *To All the Boys I've Loved Before* trilogy (2018–2021) and *The Half of It* (2020), all have a white lead alongside an ESEA one. Otherness is not allowed unless whiteness is present to validate it, whiteness makes the Asian characters' love real and worthwhile. Are we not allowed to love, unless it is to be in love with whiteness? *Always Be My Maybe* (2019) starring Ali Wong and Randall Park is one movie that breaks this mould – and it also has the most excellent cameo from Keanu Reeves. And, of course, *Crazy Rich Asians* also celebrates Asian love. But are these the exceptions that prove the rule? Yes, because they received such large, positive response. We are so starved of (mainstream) validation, of being allowed to love *each other*, that these two films highlight what the norm is: our otherness.

There is such a dearth of ESEA stories being told on

bigger platforms within a British and Western context,* and there are so few ESEA creatives with the clout and financial success of Ms Johansson, that every detail is put under a microscope. We feel the need to fight for our own histories to be seen, for our own bodies to be represented on screen, in the pages of books and on stage.

But these representations of 'us' gets darker when we start to look outside of romcoms and Scarlett Johansson action films.

'Even by the low accuracy standards of the American film industry, this is an extraordinary casting choice. Alba's coordinates for the role lie somewhere between Madame Butterfly, Disney's Pocahontas, and Papillon Soo Soo as a Vietnamese sex worker in Full Metal Jacket'.[2] This is a tweet sent on 16 January 2023 by Arthur Asseraf, an assistant professor at Cambridge University whose work focuses on colonialism and media, while watching the film *The Sleeping Dictionary*. In the film the actress Jessica Alba plays me – a 1930s version of me. The tweet questions the

---

* It is worth noting that there is, of course, rich history in film and TV within East and South East Asia – of which many shows and films are watched and enjoyed in the West. As demonstrated with the likes of *Ghost in the Shell*, Japanese films have influenced Western filmmaking, and films made in and by Hong Kong creatives are hugely popular – such as Wong Kar-wai's films, which have had global recognition. In 2024, the Kering program and the Festival de Cannes awarded the Women in Motion Emerging Talent Award to Malaysian filmmaker Amanda Nell Eu for the film *Tiger Stripes*, and the same year an animated film (*Savages*) about the Penan, Indigenous peoples of Borneo, premiered at the festival.

casting of a Latina actress playing an Iban character, but is also about the sexualised framing of this character – and, as two of the three characters referenced are of East and South East Asian heritage, it also tells us a lot about how ESEA women are/have been so often portrayed on screen and stage.

Half Iban, half British, Alba's character Selima lives in an Iban longhouse in Sarawak. She falls in love with a British officer, John Truscott, played by Hugh Dancy. Selima is to live with, and expected to sleep with, John so that he learns the local language, hence 'sleeping dictionary'. It was filmed in Sarawak in 2000 and released in 2003.

In a lot of ways, this film has made an impression on me, including the fact I was living in Sarawak when it was made and became friends with people involved in the production. Through this film and its making, I saw how the image of who I am was made for the global stage by other people. I was both thrilled by the idea that an Iban story could be told on a main stage, and confused and troubled by what the story was telling. All the local and Indigenous women were sexualised characters who fell into the role of 'other' to the white woman. It is also worth noting that the concept of a 'sleeping dictionary' is entirely fictitious. The filmmakers were inspired by the Iban tradition of ngayap, a courtship ritual where young men and women were allowed to visit each other, unsupervised, in the evening. This tradition was not anchored in sexuality or desire, but was rather about giving young people the space and time to decide if they liked each other before committing to marriage. The idea of a 'sleeping dictionary' strays so far from cultural context and fact that it becomes a creepy obsession by white male writers and directors to fantasise and fetishise the female South East Asian body for white male consumption. The film depicts an idea not of sexual freedom, but of an Indigenous sexual appetite that is presented as a cultural norm – in opposition to the Western female characters, who are chaste and 'proper'. This film was made for a Western English-speaking audience. I knew it would be seen by people I knew or would encounter, and I felt deeply uncomfortable about that. Would this film change people's perceptions of me, in a way I would have no control over?*

The 2021 film *Edge of the World* is also about Sarawak. Starring Jonathan Rhys Meyers and set in the 1840s, it tells the story of James Brooke, an ex-British soldier who becomes the 'White Rajah' of the soon-to-be Sarawak state. This film and *The Sleeping Dictionary* both frame the white protagonist as being against the colonial system. While this meets contemporary audiences' sensibilities, it might not be historically accurate. Both men are presented as white saviours who rescue the local people. In the final

---

* I do want to note that many Sarawakians were involved in the making of the film and I don't want to take away from their input. Telling stories on a large scale, such as a film, is a constant negotiation that might not end in the way you hope.

scenes of *Edge of the World*, Rhys Meyers breathlessly says, 'to rule the jungle, I must love the jungle'. Colonialism becomes an eat, pray, love moment for the hero in action.

These stories are our current stories. Colonialism and empire are embodied in our everyday, particularly for actors. This is not about the past, it is about the now. The actor Vera Chok, who played the character of Honour Chen-Williams in the Channel 4 soap opera *Hollyoaks*, says: 'I am a colonised being – body and mind – and I move through and exist in white spaces every day, in person, and on screen, as an actor, in fictional worlds written by mostly white people. I feel almost constantly at risk, and defensive in what I consider unsafe spaces. I believe it's possible to acknowledge the colonised status without being emotional about it. I am, however, often emotional about it.

'The accent I use on a daily basis in the UK, the behaviour I consider polite and acceptable, this is a confusing mishmash of what my Anglophilic mother fiercely impressed upon me in order to appear "civilised", and in direct opposition to the way many of my more Malaysian friends and relatives live their daily lives. Do I think they are less civilised? The colonised part of my brain says yes, but the Malaysian in me longs to be MORE Malaysian. I am keenly aware of this double standard/tension.'

It is a constant conflict. The colonised body is shown repetitively through war and sex in films and other art forms. The imagined singular East and South East Asian identity has been portrayed this way in film for so long that it is now an ingrained reference point. Panthea Lee, a Taiwanese Canadian writer, notes that the up-setting and racist phrase 'little brown fucking machines powered by rice' was first used during the Philippine–American war in the late 1800s, a moment where the country was brutalised by war and native communities were forced to work in labour they hadn't before, such as sex work.³ Filipino American filmmaker and academic Celine Parreñas Shimizu writes about how this phrase got shortened to simply LBFM, and printed on T-shirts in US military bases across South East Asia. The systematically degrading way in which American military personnel interacted with ESEA women reduced them to objects, and has filtered through into media. 'Love you long time,' says a sex worker character, played by Papillon Soo, in the 1987 war film *Full Metal Jacket*, set during the Vietnam War.⁴

I write about these representations of ESEA people, and in particular women, in film for a few reasons. For one, my mother banned television in our house when I was between the ages of six and sixteen, and after we only had this tiny little square box that sat in the corner of the living room, with no furniture pointing towards it. This added another thing that made me different from my (all white) friends. Therefore, anything on the screen has this pull over me, and movies were An Event. The stories told in this format were *cool*, they were the epitome of what culture was, what I wanted to be part of. The second reason I write about these representations is because they are the mainstream. This platform is how stories are told across borders, across time, and become anchored into culture until they become culture itself.

But it isn't just film that has had a huge impact on cultural narratives. Before the screen, there was the stage.

This theme of ESEA women as sexual convenience for military men is most famously portrayed in the opera *Madama Butterfly*,* which premiered in Milan in 1904. This opera tells of a US navy officer who marries a fifteen-year-old Japanese girl Cio-Cio San, before finding a 'proper' white American wife. Cio-Cio San eventually kills herself.

Jane Monari is an opera singer based in Glasgow, and is fourth-generation Japanese American ('my family is very culturally American'). 'A lot of opera stories are told from a deeply colonial eighteenth-century perspective. I think there are better ways to tell the stories, and there are better, more updated stories that we can tell,' Jane says to me. Within the whiteness of opera though, the way in which these stories are told is just as important as the stories themselves. Jane notes that it was only in 2022 that the Royal Opera House cast a Black Otello, 'which is wild,' she says. 'Almost 150 years after it was written, you decide maybe it's time for a Black man to play a role

---

* This is based on a short story ('Madame Butterfly') by American author John Luther Long, published in 1898 and based on his sister's memories of living in Japan with her husband, who was a Christian missionary.

written for a Black man? I would like East Asian people to be played by East Asian people,' she says. If there aren't such opera singers any available, Jane suggests a concert production with an orchestra only, without costumes. 'Or just don't do *Madama Butterfly* – do a Tosca instead!'

In a Twitter thread in relation to *Madama Butterfly* and a 2022 production by the Royal Opera House, Jane explains that 'yellowface' is not just about make up. It is about wigs and costumes, and 'most essentially, putting people in the wrong roles. Yellowface is pretending to be a race that you're not.'

'Opera uses colour-blind casting, but it is done thinking of casting as a two-way street. So they [those in positions to cast] think, "Oh, if we can cast non-white people in roles written for a European identity, then we can cast white people in roles for people of colour." I've had a very difficult time trying to explain to people that that's not how that works. Opera is just so behind the times, like, it's embarrassing,' Jane says. The issue with colour-blind casting is that even with a diverse cast, you strip away the ability to look into the nuances and tensions of race and culture. But when there is a lack of diversity in an industry to begin with, colour-blind casting brings us back to the Scarlett Johansson dilemma.

The musical *Miss Saigon*, which premiered in London in 1989, retells *Madama Butterfly*, this time against the backdrop of the Vietnam War. It has been hugely popular since its first production, touring and attracting audiences around the world. The original British production team held auditions for the lead role of Kim only in Manila, which academic Tzu-I Chung links to the American colonial relationship with the Philippines. The Philippines' schooling system is in English, plus has a system called 'bodabil' where plays are staged in English with popular American songs, which Chung explains as being 'powerful cultural tools' that familiarise Filipinos with an American lifestyle.[5] I think this provides a sense of distancing from the subject matter of the Vietnam War, combined with a homogenising of South East Asian identity that allows *Miss Saigon* to then be exoticised, right from its beginning.

The Crucible Theatre in Sheffield put on a production of *Miss Saigon* in the summer of 2023. The play *WORTH*, a story about a British Chinese family written, directed and performed by ESEA people, was to be on tour at Sheffield theatres during the same period. However, the creative company behind *WORTH* pulled out. 'The damaging tropes, misogyny and racism inherent in the show [*Miss Saigon*] completely contradict New Earth and Storyhouse's [the production company] values and beliefs,' said the team in a statement.[6] The director of *WORTH*, Mingyu Lin, explained to me, 'it became clear from personal accounts brought forward that ESEA artists were voicing a sense of unease and lack of safety about being at Sheffield concurrent to *Miss Saigon*. I felt that my personal responsibility was to look out for the well-being of the creatives I'm in charge of.' Beats.org, a non-profit advocacy organisation representing East and South East

Asians in the stage and screen industries, also released a statement about the production of *Miss Saigon* and the musical's role in perpetuating a racist and hyper-sexualised narrative of South East Asian women.[7] Sheffield Theatres responded with a statement, claiming their production would be akin to a retelling of a classic.[8] It is also worth noting that Sheffield Theatres receives public funding.

I agree with Jane Monari – there *are* better stories to be told. I don't think *Madama Butterfly* or *Miss Saigon* are stories that need to be told at all. They are taking up space for these other stories. A story is never a singular narrative. It is part of a wider canon. Creators making these decisions need to ask themselves – what story are you telling? How does it feed into a wider narrative? Vera Chok says, 'If you *must* do *Miss Saigon* [or the like], then you must have auxiliary shows and events around it that show the reason why you're doing it, what you're inter-rogating, and fully acknowledge the problematic nature of the piece.' These additional events would need to be built into and announced alongside the show, so as to demonstrate the interrogation and public discussion. (It is worth noting that Vera couldn't think of a reason why anyone *must* do *Miss Saigon*.)

Summer 2023 also saw the premiere of *untitled f*ck m*ss s**gon play*, written by Asian American playwright Kimber Lee. It was a joint production between the Royal Exchange, Manchester International Festival, the Young Vic and Headlong Theatre (a production company). This play traverses time and media of a similar genre, starting at *Madama Butterfly*, working its way through *South Pacific*, *M*A*S*H* and *Miss Saigon* (of course), picking up stereotypes of the Asian woman character as it goes. The play lampoons the narrative – the perfect 'Asian' woman is abandoned, and then kills herself. But in its repetition, it is painful, and it is hysterically and heartbreakingly funny. It is also so, so cringe. It is too real. I know these lines, and I winced as I laughed. The play's end setting is in 2023 and, ultimately, it tells the story of how these repeated stories become embodied in us. They become generational trauma and we live them. It was an important play, but it was an American play – its last scenes were set in New York, and the British actors had American accents. I was left wanting to know, where were our stories? Where were the stories of British ESEA people? Why weren't British playwrights being commissioned for these spaces? The stories we watch and tell define us, how we see ourselves and how we are seen.

Jennifer Tang is an award-winning theatre director, and was a Genesis Fellow* (a two-year grant that allows the recipient to be an associate director at the Young Vic). 'There's definitely still an ingrained sense that making, for example, an East or South East Asian narrative is a niche piece of work that will only appeal to ESEA theatregoers, which is fucking bonkers,' she says. 'And additionally, if you look at audience demographics, your ESEA audience is not one of the biggest. So people think, how do we

---

*   At the time of my interview with her.

broaden this out? Well, then you probably need an East meets West story, because at least the audience identify with one story.' Jennifer laughs at this, with a slight eye-roll.

When I ask Jennifer about her own story, she prefaces it by saying, 'this is what I believe to be true. If it's 100 per cent factually accurate, I don't know. There are massive holes.' Jennifer, who is Chinese and born in the UK, tells me how she was fostered when ten days old by a white family, in what she believes was supposed to be a short-term arrangement but which became permanent. Her white mother and father were not her legal guardians, as her mother didn't want to sign any official documents. Jennifer's mother worked at a Chinese restaurant and so the hours were probably not conducive to having a newborn baby. Three years later, Jennifer's brother was born and came to live with them too. Jennifer believes her maternal grandfather came over from the New Territories under the visa opportunities for Hong Kong and New Territories people in the 1970s; he opened a takeaway in Gravesend, Kent. As a teenager, Jennifer legally changed her name, giving up her Chinese name, which she now looks back on and understands the hurt that must have caused her mother, but was a decision she felt was necessary at the time. She was the first in her families – both her Chinese and white family – to go to university.

As you can imagine, this is barely touching the sides of Jennifer's personal story. And I tell it here, in a brief recap,* because I am excited that she is one of the emerging leading voices in British theatre. Her understanding of home, belonging, identity, the complication of personal histories and simply how to tell stories is so layered that her lens is, and always will be, wide. I have no doubt that with the future of theatre in her hands – and so many others – we will be able to have complex stories told with empathy and interrogation. It feels exciting. There is simply no reason to be retelling old stories by white men. 'What I think will happen, as artistic directors change, and they [theatres] stop being white-dominated and patriarchal spaces . . . then the programming lens will get wider,' Jennifer says.

Theatres in the UK are huge organisations. They are housed in culturally important buildings and are recipients of public arts funding. The stories that are told in them are vital to our understanding of British-ness. And the theatre is a place I found a home in, which is also why I feel so personally and deeply invested in the stories we tell, and how they are told onstage.

I co-founded the theatre company 'Behind the Bikeshed' in 2007 with Nicola Young, another woman of New Zealand Asian heritage, and Ben Roberts, a white

---

* I couldn't do Jennifer's story justice in the pages of this book; this is true for all the people I have spoken to. I hope everyone will find their own ways to tell their story, if they wish. I merely touch on these stories, hopefully respectfully, to show how incredible complex the idea of ESEA identity is in the UK.

Australian man. The company ran for nine years, and throughout that time, we gathered people, building a little community of writers, performers and artists. This wasn't a community that was focused on identity, but it was a space where a huge range of conversations could happen. We had to cast against gender or race because our company was mainly made up of women, and we had a range of different cultural and ethnic backgrounds. We did find that no matter the writer, scripts were always written with character descriptions of 'white,' and/or 'male', when they really didn't need to be, showing just how ingrained this 'norm' is in all of us.

For others, the theatre has also been a space for exploring personal and collective identity and finding a voice. Over the years, Daniel York Loh, associate artistic director of Kakilang Arts and co-founder of Moongate Productions,* also found a home in theatre, but it was hard work to find that space, that home. 'It was because of the career I chose that I became aware of racialising. If I had become an accountant, I'm not sure it would have been an issue. When I left drama school, I became a "Chinese actor".' Daniel, who is half white and half Chinese, says. Although he experienced horrific racism as a child, it wasn't a cultural identity that he associated with. But because of this labelling, he had to find a way to become connected to his Chinese-ness. How could he be 'Chinese', and how could he be a 'Chinese actor'?

---

* Both companies look to platform ESEA stories in the UK.

Daniel's father had come over to the UK from Singapore as a child with his mother and (white) stepfather. Daniel's father's and Daniel's own childhood weren't centred on Chinese culture. 'We didn't celebrate Lunar New Year, I don't think I ever went to a Chinese restaurant until I was an adult. The only Chinese food we ate was from a Chinese takeaway; my grandmother had two friends ("uncle" and "auntie") and they had a Chinese takeaway. "Uncle" would cook food for us, it tasted amazing at the time and my grandma and auntie would stand in the kitchen talking Cantonese, and I used to be mesmerised by them. They were just incredible, magical creatures to me.'

The first play Daniel was in post-drama school changed his life. 'It was about race and racism, and Glen [Goei] – who wrote and directed it – had been in *M Butterfly.** He was the only East Asian person I had seen in a play. He was Singaporean too.' But, interestingly, when auditioning for TV roles ('terrible parts') Daniel would never be cast because he wasn't 'Chinese enough' and of course he wasn't 'white enough' to play white roles. It wasn't Daniel making decisions on his identity, his identity was up to others. It is because of this that he has leant into theatre work. And so, in contrast, theatre has been a space that has allowed Daniel to explore identity and where he isn't 'not enough'; he has written, performed and produced a

---

* A play written by David Henry Hwang that subverts many of the racial and sexualised tropes of *Madama Butterfly*.

CHINESE AND ANY OTHER ASIAN

variety of plays, including roles and stories that dive deep into Chinese identity, culture and history.

Because of having to navigate his identity in the public space of stage and screen, Daniel questions what representation is and what it can do. 'There's an expression called RepresentAsian, which is all about "are we in Hollywood?" But is that real politics? Is that real racial equality? How actually race conscious are we? How conscious are we of anti-Blackness? Of colourism in our own communities? I have to say, generally, when you look at us as a collection of diasporic groups, but dominated I think in the West by East Asians, our race politics are not very good.' This brings us back to the beginning of this chapter, and makes me think about what representations we are looking for. If our identity is defined by others, how do we advocate for representation of ourselves, and for diversity of our stories?

I wanted to know what Vera Chok felt about these ideas of representation, given that she has worked across theatre, television and film. She tells me, 'I am more interested in the term "inclusion". True representation is impossible – it is impossible to show all facets of any one individual's life, let alone of an entire marginalised group because we are not a homogenous lump.

'Full inclusion is also impossible, but an effort to include the historically excluded into a space, a conversation, feels more like an acknowledgement of their specificity, an invitation for their participation, and less an assertion of "We are going to represent you"/"You being here means we 'have' representation." Inclusion feels active, and representation feels somehow diminishing or condescending. I think a useful question to ask is always, "Who isn't in the room, and why?" Also not to beat ourselves up if we can't get everyone in the room.'

This idea of inclusion, of an invitation to join in, rings so true to me and encompasses how I feel about various creative experiences I have been privileged to be part of in the last few years. I have been working specifically with ESEA artists on a quest to workshop, collaborate and exchange ideas. In October 2022, I was lucky enough to be invited by Omar Musa, an Australian Borneo artist, to perform poetry alongside him and others – this was an evening at Spiritland, a music-focused bar in the Southbank in London, specifically curated by Omar. It was amazing to perform my work next to someone who knew my South East Asian Indigenous world and was also writing and performing around similar themes – I didn't feel the need to explain myself. And, in 2021, I was invited to two different artist residencies, which both had a performance slant to them. These experiences were liberating because of the women who participated and because of the women who organised and facilitated them.

In the spring of 2021, I found myself sitting in a room with other East and South East Asian women from creative and academic backgrounds, in the estate of

Hawkwood* in the Cotswolds for a weeklong residency. We were Kimvi, Georgina Quach, Tian Ma, Youngsook Choi, Elisabeth Gunawan, Jennifer Tang and artist extraordinaire Moi Tran, who organised and curated the week. Across that week, we took up space. Unashamedly. And in that British garden in the Cotswolds we seemed so out of place that it felt rebellious to even be there. On that first day, we sat cross-legged in a circle, looking out of wide windows into the English countryside, and Moi said: to build a canon, we all have to reference each other.

Moi was born in Quảng Ninh province, Vietnam before leaving with her family as refugees, exiled due to her grandfather's ethnic Chinese heritage. 'In Vietnam, this part of history is sensitive and is seldom discussed, at times even refuted,' Moi says. 'But hundreds of thousands of Vietnamese people were forced to flee, risking their lives on unsafe fishing boats. Many perished on the seas, unable to see land again.' Moi and her family lived in refugee camps in Hong Kong for a few years before coming to the UK in 1980, and they eventually settled in London, where a Vietnamese community was beginning to gather.

Moi's work encompasses many avenues, she has a fine art practice in parallel to working as a designer in various platforms in live performance, such as theatre, opera and dance. 'At this point in my practice, I prefer

---

* This estate is the Hawkwood Centre for Future Thinking, which is a charity to support creative endeavour and community work.

not to be bracketed and it feels reductive,' she explains. Moi explains that she fought her way into the arts, 'and I continue to do so.' Growing up, she didn't have access to the arts, and so her path to creating art included detours and a constant questioning on practice and identity. Moi now sees this as a way to flourish and nurture curiosity, which seems so clear in her organising of our residency retreat: 'I wanted to enjoy and celebrate the witnessing of ESEA people flourishing in each other's company, to build and share knowledge, to imagine collective futures, surrounded by the beauty of nature,' Moi says.

Similarly, in September 2021, I was invited by Nur Khairiyah Bte Ramli (Khai) to be part of the project Kelab Malam, produced by her company RUMAH (Rumah means 'home' in Malay). I was joined by Mae Williams, of Filipino supperclub fame, and KG Patarita Tassanarapan, a Thai artist and chef. During our residency, we mapped all the places we have called home onto the black rehearsal-room floor. We built a table with banana leaves, sarongs and batik fabrics across the floor; we layered on to it not food, but the ingredients we love. Around this table, we placed nine 'settings' of objects that anchored us to ideas of home and we invited friends into this space. It was beautiful and I really wish you were all there.

Khai is a Muslim, Malay, Singaporean. She set up RUMAH to 'reimagine a space for artists from various Asian diasporas in Britain to integrate and collaborate'. She arrived in the UK with her husband, Mohamad Faizal Abdullah, to do MAs in Theatre. She originally thought she would be a housewife, 'sort of tagging along', which is amusing to me as Khai is a born organiser, instigator and thought-leader. In London, Khai has found ways to feel at home. When it comes to food, London feels diverse: 'We are asked about allergies, dietary requirements, and accommodations can be made where necessary – you can find many halal restaurants here in London,' she explains to me.

Within work, Khai navigates a predominantly white theatre world. 'I do feel that I've been given a seat on the table, because I have asked for it. It's not a natural thing for them [people of power within theatre organisations] to think my voice or opinion is relevant,' she says. It feels like a diversity tick box. 'I am other Asian, I am female, I am Muslim. That's at least three diversity boxes ticked,' Khai tells me. This is why RUMAH is so important; it gives visibility for ESEA groups. But Khai does feel under-represented under the ESEA banner.

She explains to me that very few people really understand Singapore, and even less the Malay identity within Singapore. Khai tells me that even within the Singapore diaspora, there isn't a lot of acknowledgement or knowledge of Muslim Malay people: 'I got invited to a Singaporean gathering in London and was told the restaurant was not halal. That's fine, I am used to it. But if it's a Singaporean gathering, organised by "my fellow countrymen", you would think that the organisers would know that there are people of difference races, cultures and faiths with different dietary requirements. Not just for

Muslims, but for Hindus, Buddhists, etc.,' she explained. For example, there was only one vegetarian dish. The experience made her feel like a token Muslim, Malay in a large Chinese Singaporean event.

'The portrayal of Singapore is very singular unfortunately – I blame the Singapore Tourism Board, and *Crazy Rich Asians*.' Discussing identity, religion and cultural identity with Khai is also important – and complex, and difficult – because of the continued rise in Islamophobia, demonstrating the crucial need to understand ESEA identity with nuance and as a multiple; to give space for multiple voices and identities.

This book, in many ways, is an ode to Moi's statement, to build our own canon. Our communities' expertise is wide, deep and varied. We each have the power to create a new canon, a new understanding of knowledge and the world around us. That begins by referencing each other, by trusting in our expertise and building step by step.

These two experiences in 2021 taught me about this need to be with other people with similar backgrounds and histories to mine, to build community and connection, and to value those women who are organising and facilitating space. It is here that our stories are heard, told and witnessed. From here, we are able to craft stories that will change the cultural narratives.

Finding stories of us, for us, by us is a quest that goes beyond the stage and screens. The most powerful stories we can consume are the ones that are intimate. The words on a page and songs in our headphones on a Sony Walkman, on an iPod, on your phone. When I think of my childhood and teenage years, it is of losing myself in books and listening to tapes I had saved up to buy. Both activities gave me a space to imagine, but I do look back and wish that there was more 'me' in those spaces and that I wasn't constantly trying to insert myself into book pages or music lyrics.

With music, I was always drawn to the more outspoken and political. The first tape I bought myself was *Les Misérables* (I said outspoken, I didn't mean 'cool'), stomping around the house, humming the tune of 'Do You Hear the People Sing?' This then moved on to a more punk approach – Rage Against the Machine and Skunk Anansie were key, and I realise a big part of it was that these musicians were people of colour. I was craving to see something else, something 'other'.

Growing up in New Zealand, naturally I listened to Bic Runga, and clung to everything she did. As a half Maori and half Chinese Malaysian, she was an approximation of me. I remember reading that she lived in Paris and London – she was painfully cool. Back in Sarawak one summer holiday, I scoured the music shops and asked about English-speaking female artists. Here, I found Anggun, an Indonesian French singer whose 1998 album *Snow on the Sahara* I listened to on repeat. She too lived in France and England – these daring, international, *cool* women with South East Asian backgrounds, there was hope for me yet!

Karen O of the Yeah Yeah Yeahs was Asian American, and she was *rock*. This was my music (my other dream job would've been to be a rock star, although I fear playing the flute was the wrong route). O wasn't very vocal about her heritage (from what I saw) and she shouldn't have to be. But it was something I was looking for, which is why I was particularly drawn to Anggun singing in Indonesian, as well as English and French – she was clear about her heritage. The only previous East or South East Asian woman in music I had reference to was Yoko Ono, and all I really knew about her was that she wasn't regarded well. It took years for me to realise the racist misogyny of that narrative.

With the astronomic rise of K-pop bands, East Asian faces do feel more familiar now in the global music scene. And in May 2021, something happened that my teen-age punk self could have only dreamt about. The teenage band The Linda Lindas went viral with their punk song 'Racist, Sexist Boy', performed at the Los Angeles Public Library. The lyrics are everything we could hope for – to the point, calling the protagonist a racist and sexist, rhyming boy with joy, and explaining the how racism and sexism can be damaging. The group is made up of Eloise Wong, cousin to sisters Lucia and Mila de la Garza, and friend Bela Salazar; they explain that the band is 'half Latinx and half Asian'.

In the summer of 2023, I saw Griff, the British singer-songwriter of Vietnamese and Jamaican heritage who won Rising Star at the 2021 Brit Awards, on stage at All Points

East festival. She owned the stage and joked about how her decision to get acrylic nails the day before had ruined her ability to now play the guitar as planned. In the US, Mitski, a Japanese American singer-songwriter, had one of the biggest global hits of 2023 with her ballad 'My Love Mine All Mine'.

During her 2023 Glastonbury set, British Japanese pop star Rina Sawayama said 'I wrote this next song ['STFU'] because I was sick and tired of microaggressions. So, tonight, this song goes out to a white man who watches Ghetto Gaggers* and mocks Asian people on a podcast. He also owns my masters. I've had enough.'† It is believed to be referring to Matty Healy,‡ lead singer of the band The 1975, who was accused of mocking rapper Ice Spice, incorrectly identifying her (among other things) as Chinese while appearing on a US podcast (he later gave an onstage apology for offending Ice Spice[9]). The podcast episode also included imitations of Chinese, Hawaiian and Japanese accents for laughs and was pulled after a few months, following the backlash.

Sawayama criticised the BRIT Awards when her 2020 self-titled album was deemed ineligible for the BRITs and

---

*   Ghetto Gaggers is an extreme porn site that degrades women of colour, which Adam Friedland alleged that Healy has watched.
†   Healy was a creative director of Dirty Hit, the record label Sawayama is signed with, from 2019 until April 2023.
‡   As reported by various publications, including *Rolling Stone* (25 June 2023), the *Guardian* (24 June 2023) and the *Independent* (25 June 2023).[10]

Mercury Prize because she doesn't have British citizenship, despite living in the UK from the age of four. She retains her Japanese citizenship to keep ties with family as Japan doesn't recognise dual citizenship. In 2021, her campaigning and a meeting with British Phonographic Industry (who organise both awards) culminated in a change of regulations – those who have been a resident in the UK for over five years now qualify; on a Twitter post she wrote: 'REDEFINING BRITISHNESS !!!!!! shoutout @bpi_music !!!!!'[11] Sawayama is also a member of ESEA Music, a UK non-profit group started in September 2021, which provides support and aims to raise awareness. In 2023 they conducted a survey, named (Re) Orientated, with approximately eighty of its members; the survey highlighted ESEA under-representation in the music industry.

The space ESEA artists take up in the music world, in particular the UK, is still small and at times incredibly frustrating, but change does seem to be happening and their voices are beginning to be being heard.

But along with this flow of the new storytellers of our generation – music, theatre, film, books (more of which later) – there are reminders of what is the status quo. These new works seem revolutionary because they are against a backdrop of the previous narratives, and as *Miss Saigon* demonstrates, these narratives are still here. So often art and culture – the films, plays, operas, musicals – are stories of far-off places, for the consumption of the West. They allow the audience to travel to 'exotic' locations. They are travel writing made physical, and travel writing can be a really troublesome space. These narratives often conflate and package people and places up as a commodity to be consumed by the outsider, often those with the wealth and privilege to be able to travel there. Like *Miss Saigon et al.* and in travel writing, our stories are so often written by white people; not just our stories, but where we call home and our cultural heritage.

Jan Morris was an historian who – as well as many other things – wrote travelogue-style pieces about Hong Kong. She was incredibly acclaimed, and the *Guardian*'s obituary stated she 'evoked time and place with the flair of a novelist'.[12] (She died in 2020 and, as well as the *Guardian*, she had obituaries in the *Financial Times*, the *New York Times* and other leading papers). But in her book *Hong Kong: Epilogue to an Empire*, which was printed in 1988 and reprinted in 1997 to coincide with the handover, she wrote: 'From the beginning Hong Kong seems to have been more prurient even than most such colonial settlements, partly because of the climate perhaps, partly because *European males have always been attracted by nubile Chinese females*, partly because the early settlers were often men of vigorous appetite and flexible morals, and partly because the air of Hong Kong somehow seems to suggest that in sex, as in most other things, anything goes.'[13] Italics my own, because this part of the sentence shocked me so much, and also because it is key in understanding how the West viewed East Asian women specifically, but generally framed non-white women.

To understand this quote, as well as why this way of writing about Hong Kong was not only tolerated but enjoyed, it is important to understand the cultural relationship of Hong Kong and Britain. As one of the last imperial outposts, Hong Kong become a performance of empire. Within this, a narrative of 'unbridled capitalism' is told, which links to a masculinity and sexualisation of women, academic Mark Hampton explained to me. This wasn't just demonstrated by travel writing about the city, but also in the way the handover was portrayed in the UK. The *Sun*'s now-defunct topless 'Page Three girl',* published on the day of handover in 1997, was a British-born Chinese model of Hong Kong heritage. The caption read: 'Here's a little Hong Kong phewy to mark today's transfer of the colony to Beijing rule – 23-year-old Ivy Yeung, whose parents are Chinese. Of course, our new Page 3 girl, who lives in the Lake District, would be worth Peking at ANY day. Just look what she has her handover [her breasts]'.†

---

* The Page Three/Page 3 is a British tradition in red-top tabloids. The *Sun* last published a topless Page 3 model on 22 January 2015, the *Daily Star* continued until 2019.
† I discovered Morris' writing and the detail about the *Sun* through a book by Mark Hampton, which was a critical look at the cultural relationship between Hong Kong and the UK – *Hong Kong and British Culture, 1945–97* – and then interviewed Mark further on specific points from this book.[14]

During the twentieth century, Hong Kong held an unusual place within the British psyche. It had been a transitional place, but after the Second World War, there was a growing and stable Chinese population. Coupled with the looming handover date, there was an idea – at least for foreigners – to enjoy the party while it lasted. Mark also points out that the performance of capitalism, and with it the excess and masculinity, was against China's communist ideology.

When reading Morris's book in the British Library, it made me feel sick to my stomach. As so many had before her, she was painting a picture of ESEA women as hyper-sexualised. At the same time, she robbed them of their agency. I recognised this language and it is why I can't see cultural spaces – from theatres to restaurants – where ownership is white and particularly male, where they are selling a story of fun, party and a foreign location, without seeing exoticism. It is the same story. It is coding the idea of 'Asia' and its people as pleasure and for consumption. It is not just a personal reaction. It is an analysis of how the idea of Asia has been perpetuated and sold to the West and white audiences within a capitalist structure. This is structural racism, stories to titillate a white audience with an idea of adventure, and it makes me cry in the British Library.

As a child, I found solace in books. My favourite place was the library, it was a haven. But growing up, there weren't a lot of books I read that featured people who looked like me, sounded like me, had my experiences. I found home in fantasy stories because at least the idea of difference was core to so much. But it does feel like a change is happening. I have been asked to curate a book club list, one devoted to Asian literature, and I am excited about how many ESEA authors I am able to add to that list.

If we look globally, there are those of East and South East Asian heritage writing massive global hits – such as Korean American musician Michelle Zauner's hit memoir *Crying in H Mart* (2021) – which had me crying on a beach, in an airplane, on a train – and *Tomorrow and Tomorrow and Tomorrow* (2022) by US author Gabrielle Zevin, who is of mixed Korean heritage, and whose novel, which includes two main characters of ESEA heritage, is breaking records. Shelley Parker-Chan's books, *She Who Became the Sun* (2021) and *He Who Drowned the World* (2023), are queer retellings of fourteenth-century China and the end of the Mongol Empire. The novels have won awards across the world; and Parker-Chan is Australian, with Malaysian Chinese heritage. And the global industry's darling R.F. Kuang can't seem to put pen to paper without writing a bestseller and gathering fans.

And in the UK, there is a growing group of writers gathering recognition. Angela Hui's memoir, *Takeaway: Stories from a Childhood Behind the Counter* (2022), tells of growing up in a Chinese takeaway in a village in Wales. The book was shortlisted for a number of awards, such as the Fortnum & Mason Debut Food Book Award and the Jhalak Prize, and was one of Waterstones' Best Paperbacks of 2023. A heartfelt memoir, it tells a story that is both familiar to British people – the local Chinese takeaway, a feature in the landscape of Britain, both rural and city – and yet, is so hidden and unknown. Behind that counter are the stories that have not been given time and space till now. This book felt important, as well as being beautiful storytelling to sink your literary teeth into.

Kaliane Bradley is of Cambodian heritage, and her debut book, *The Ministry of Time* (2024), is set in London. Through a sci-fi story, it delves into identity, as well as mystery, danger and histories, and is one of my favourite books. Claire Kohda's first book, *Woman, Eating* (2022), traces the story of a mixed-race vampire artist trying to make it in the art world of London. Claire, who is of mixed Japanese heritage, weaves a story of finding self and the ideas of hunger and desire.

Books allow us to reimagine our own stories because we can picture ourselves in the scenarios on the page. We get to construct the spaces, we get to be active in these storytellings. To me, this allows for a space of joy, even if we are navigating trauma. How these new narratives are showing a sense of reclaiming identity, a way to exist in the world, feels totally punk to me – it's not tidy, not well-behaved. The power of storytelling is to give power.

Cecile Pin's book *Wandering Souls* (2023) gives this power through the act of retelling history. It is a fictional story of Vietnamese refugees and the protagonist says: 'I want magic powers for the armless and harmless. I want a John Wick-style revenge on their executioners.' But one line has stuck with me, the character also says 'The truth is, I don't want to write about death. I want women to live.'[15]

Will Harris's essay book *Mixed-Race Superman* (2018) also expresses the messiness. He delves into understanding race and the confusion of mixed-race-ness, and looks at a world that feels dangerous and divided. But, with Keanu Reeves, Barack Obama, Greek myths and pop culture as heroes, he finds ways into these discussions that get to also feel fun, and with fun comes power and joy.

I want to live in joy, I want delight. It is the continued reframing and complicating of identity I am seeing in this new (bigger?) wave of ESEA writers that is exciting and offers a new way of viewing myself, ourselves, in the world. There has got to be a meme somewhere of Keanu taking in the sadness, pain and trauma and still finding joy. Or maybe his existence is all we need. And god, how I do love the John Wick films; and it has not escaped my notice that Rina Sawayama is in *John Wick: Chapter 4*.

I have lived in a world of white stories for so long. When these stories are constantly repeated, they become part of a cultural lexicon, where East and South East Asian women are sexual objects with a backdrop of violence and white men are colonial heroes. It is impossible for this concept not to filtrate through to the everyday. The possibility to connect across cultures and history is in reality easily done. We need more East and South East Asian stories, for everyone to enjoy. Let us retire *Miss Saigon* and *Madama Butterfly*. We have abused their stories enough, we have battled over their histories, we have appropriated their identities. Let them rest. Let these women find peace. Let them be sacred and not the toys of capitalism of the white man's world.

Chapter 6

Food

When it comes to food, my absolute pet hate is the use of the word 'banging'.

A few years ago, a tweet stated that *The Nutcracker*'s 'Dance of the Sugar Plum Fairy' 'was a banging tune'. And goddammit, they were correct! The rhythm has, well, a bang to it. But when the word gets utilised to describe food, the whole mood changes. 'Banging' is often used when describing 'spicy' food, food with heat. Chilli peppers, like ginger and pepper, include a chemical make-up that is actually a touch sense, not taste – the 'heat' of these spices is physical pain. So 'banging' makes sense: a physical sensation. A physical reaction. A violent response.

What else is banging? Someone 'hot' is 'bang-able'. Describing someone flirting can be phrased as 'they were hitting on me'. When you see it in black and white, it seems so strange. Sexualised violence, in everyday language. Words change and they can lose their original meaning. But when 'banging' is continuously linked with foods made by people who've endured colonial violence, or who've had narratives of sexualised violence told about them in popular media; where the places the foods are from are spaces of colonialism, spaces with violent histories, perpetuated by mostly white men under state sanctions – it gets deeply uncomfortable. Banging guns and cannons, banging fists, all sex and war. It doesn't feel fair at all.

Jenny Lau, food writer and community organiser, and I are walking around London Fields, ruminating on this topic. 'It [banging] makes me squirm. I'm hazarding a guess that it's spread through the media of fast-casual spaces like TikTok and Instagram and I can almost guarantee that a young British wahey-ish male chef started it. I'm fascinated by the types of female foodies who have also adopted it. They tend to be young, Cool Girl-adjacent, probably have aspirations to be considered as low-key hot and super chill at the same time. Everyone on MOB Kitchen uses it. Am I being judgmental and snarky? You bet I am!'

Both of us are overthinkers and would never actually police the use of this word to get it 'cancelled'. But we hate it. For all its violent and racialised connotations.

Jenny also makes a connection with music. 'The other new food lingo that irks me is "that slaps". When you think about it, "banging" and "that slaps" are both colloquial phrases that migrated over from music slang. "It/ that slaps" was coined by a rapper called E-40 to refer to a good bassline. I do love the way slang spills over across subcultures and genres, and in this case the direction in which it has travelled indicates something about how food media/food language has evolved and to what it aspires to – i.e. the coolness of music.' It works in music, you bang a drum, you slap your hands, it has a reference point of rhythm; but it doesn't carry over well into food, particularly when used by white people in regard to food by people of colour.

There is a performance to food, and the use of this physical-based language demonstrates that. But who is doing the labour of these performances, and who is consuming it? Jenny thinks that 'in essence, the ways in which these exogenous slang words penetrate and become acculturated into our food language are an insidious type of identity commodification. Because what sells? It's still sex and power.' And when we look at East and South East Asian food, made by East and South East Asian people, we don't often see power. But we can see sex, dressed up in the trope of the exotic, where white creators use East and South East Asia as a backdrop for their food, especially in the storytelling of restaurants.

Food is the focal point of a restaurant, to be examined and appraised. In communities that have a robust food culture, the dissection of dishes is an act of bonding, of creating memory and building connection to a space and time and place. 'We eat to remember place,' anthropologist David Sutton explains to me in an interview for my podcast, *Taste of Place*.*[1] Restaurants have a history and an

---

* Sutton's work looks at the how food plays a part in create place and identity, his research is predominantly based on the Greek island of Kalymnos.

anchor in the idea of being spaces of restorative-ness,* of gathering and of being with people, of nourishment. But in the capitalist space and structure of (for example) the London restaurant scene, there are competing threads of intention: aesthetics is key, entertainment is paramount, nostalgia runs riot. And social media is the lens. Therefore, food culture and restaurants take on a different role and become performative of wider cultural narratives where the identity of the other is for sale.

One evening I watched the launch of a white-founded South East Asian-inspired restaurant through my phone. In a society which has a robust social media culture, the detailed look at the fleeting stories on Instagram is a natural medium to consume and dissect a restaurant. I watched as a Thai band performed to a mostly white crowd, who mostly ignored them. They were dressed-up, shimmering, moving wallpaper. To be looked at, and disregarded; that was what the smartphone-shot video story told. I am sure the band had agency in this performance – that they were paid well and had a good time. But I can't help but react.

The images, these short videos made by individuals and reshared by the restaurant, hit my stomach and gave me a visceral reaction that I don't know if I even have the words to express well. I am reminded of when I didn't have agency. When I put on a pretty dress and went out

---

* The word 'restaurant' comes from the French verb 'restaurer', which means to restore or re-establish.

into the world and was treated like flesh. To be consumed. Eyes eating, words coating me to make me small; when I was still a teenager, still just a child. My understanding of sexuality has always been understood in terms of race and racism. A body in space, for others. In my forties, I am still untangling ideas of desire, both mine and others, from racism. These images all remind me of this.

Anyone can cook anything, can start any business, and can do it well. But do they need to do it? This was the question I kept asking myself.

I was watching white men be nostalgic for a version of Asia they remember from their twenties: either their gap year, or their first grown-up holiday. It is awkward at best, deeply triggering at worst. The pissed-up nights of Brits Abroad: Lads in Bangkok vibe is layered with something a little bit grim. Power imbalances, sexual connotations, expectations. Boys will be boys but at whose cost? This has been reimagined in Central London. Also central is our very own Chinatown; a place where East and South East Asian people are losing their businesses, being priced out. I'm not writing this to question whether this restaurant should exist, but rather thinking about power and who gets to thrive. Who gets to have a business with a fancy launch party?

My stomach turns. And I read how the food is being described by some guests as 'banging'.

Not only is 'spicy' a stand-in for chilli heat, it also seems to be a stand-in for 'authentic'. The use of this term eradicates the idea of nuance in the food from this South

East Asian region. Authentic means hot; hotter, hottest.
It's masculine in tone, it's colonial in feel – consuming
the heat of the East, meeting the challenge of that heat.
Conquering it.

Conquering.

Banging.

There are ESEA people and other people of colour at
the restaurant launch, posting on social media as well.
The London restaurant world isn't an entirely racist one.
I have no doubt many enjoyed the evening; we are not a
homogenous group. I also suspect that many didn't, but
posted anyway – it was a launch party, it was all free and
that is the economy of launch etiquette.

My perspective and life experience will lead me to have
certain reactions and readings of a situation, so I know
that others won't have felt the same seeing this. I doubt
this restaurant will struggle, so my thoughts are incon-
sequential. But as I scanned the restaurant's social media
feed, I saw details of the dishes and drinks served but an
absence of story about the band as artists or people; the
Instagram stories don't name them as a band, let alone
as individuals. It feels to me like they are just bodies for
the entertainment of the (mostly white) guests. I don't
see the details of the people that adorn the walls, just
photos of brown bodies in picture frames, dressed up to
be visually consumed by a Western audience. There is a
film about a place that inspired this cuisine. Beautifully
done, of course. Romantic lingering vistas of rivers.

For me it all adds to a dehumanisation of South East Asia. A tire company* has convinced us that food is the only bar to judge a restaurant, the rest is noise. But no amount of excellent execution of a dish is going to convince me to go to this place. To my mind it has 'but I have an Asian wife' vibes.

This restaurant is no sugar plum fairy. It ain't banging, babe.

On 8 August 2021, the London restaurant The Ivy Asia released a social media advert that depicted two East Asian women dressed as geisha, being driven around by an East Asian man in rickshaw. The clip ended with the women tumbling into the restaurant to be stared at by white patrons. The social media response was instant. The criticism was clear and the ESEA community broke down the dangers of racist stereotypes and creating homogenous representation and reductive characters for the amusement of white people. The following day Caprice Holdings, who owned the Ivy Asia, offered an apology of sorts.† This incident was interesting; off the back of what had been happening over the previous eighteen months – from Covid-19, to the Black Lives Matter movement, and many

---

*　The Michelin Guide doesn't even bring service into consideration until it is thinking of awarding three stars, the focus is always on the food, without context.

†　The apology explained they had a 'complete ignorance of under-standing' and promised the company would educate itself to ensure it didn't happen again.[2]

new ESEA groups that developed across the country in response to the racism from Covid-19 – we found ways to cope, including to laugh at the people who could even come up with this advert. 'In terms of the community we laugh to each other, but when someone asks about it, outside of the community, it's time to act!* Because it's still triggering to think about,' Anna Chan, founder of Asian Leadership Collective, says to me.

One reaction I really enjoyed was from an Instagram and TikTok account called Don't Call Me Oriental, run by an East Asian woman called Mildred.† She posted a reel with a male voiceover saying, 'When an Asian restaurant owner is clearly not Asian,' with Mildred replicating the 'oriental' poses used by non-ESEA models in Ivy Asia's promotional art work. Made even more funnier by the fact Mildred couldn't stop laughing was the preposterous-ness of it all. She also managed, in one post, to condense the idea how conflating China the state with Chinese people leads to hate speech, in under fifteen seconds, with humour. Asians are funny, get on board.

These incidents – a racial stereotypical ad, an exoticizing restaurant launch – weren't the first, nor will be last, time racialised stereotypes are employed in restaurant settings, but they are important to think about. Restaurants are

---

* Anna explains this means: 'educating and the labour of sharing'; it's time to do this work.
† @mildredlike on Instagram.

cultural spaces and we need to see them as part of a cultural landscape and national story; therefore, what stories are they telling?

Restaurants are also places of work. So much of my adult working life has revolved around hospitality – restaurants, bars and events, primarily as a worker, and then in the last decade as a writer and researcher. I am now back working front of house at one of my favourite restaurants in London: Sambal Shiok, a laksa bar owned by my friend Mandy Yin. I love the buzz of a restaurant or bar, the camaraderie of the team – restaurants are always a place to gather the best and most interesting people a city has to offer. There can be a fun dynamic when I get to talk about food I love, to guests. I've worked in fantastic places, and Sambal Shiok in particular has been one of the safest work environments I have ever worked in. But restaurants are also where I have experienced the most racism. The combination of performance and providing a service makes the space ripe for racialised sexualisation. It always starts with 'where are you from?' before I've barely said a word. A real-life conversation I experienced:

'Where are you from?'

'London.'

'No, that's not what I mean.'

'New Zealand.'

'Oh, are you one of those Māori?'

'No' – I took the bottle of champagne and topped up

another wedding guest, looking over the rolling hills of the estate in the Midlands and sighing at how a beautiful landscape could feel so ugly.

Another time, I served a table of three middle-aged white couples, where one man moved from 'where are you from?' (accompanied by scanning my full body, as he leant back in his chair), to comments about my appearance, the heat in Malaysia and a continuous stream of innuendoes directed at me for the whole table to hear. Finally, when he was paying, I explained the card machine needed to be closer to the front to get the Wi-Fi connection and asked if he could follow me. He smiled, wiggled his eyebrows and his wife said, 'He's been waiting for you to say that all night.' This isn't a funny joke. An entire table were making me their plaything, their joke, an object to look at. I felt so worthless. A decade later, I can still see his face and the look he gave me.

Once, a very drunk white man asked me, while I tried to make him a drink: 'So, *what* are you? You don't look yellow, or brown, you look sort of . . .' and put his hand three inches from my face and made a circular movement and said 'orange'.

Of course, when it comes to food, it isn't just in service that racism is witnessed or experienced. The food itself is a point of contention and othering. During the pandemic, when we all lived online and our emotions were raw and the world seemed like a scary place, I became extremely cross at how ESEA food was being portrayed in popular media. It felt like non-ESEA cooks, chefs and TV personalities were only wanting to cook our food for a Western audience, and were behaving like *they* were the translators of these foods. When anchors of our identities, such as food, are challenged or disparaged, it can be deeply frustrating. I believe that we are allowed to feel anger when these things happen. This is an important part of negotiating how and where we fit into the cultural landscape of Britain today.

I got frustrated watching the British Thai chef John Chantarasak's food on *Great British Menu* (2020) always being framed as 'spicy', and having to meet the programme makers' palette, as opposed to his own. Cookbook author of *Dumplings and Noodles* Pippa Middlehurst used words such as 'strange' and 'alien' when describing Chinese food, across various platforms, including her website. This was originally brought to my attention by an Asian American journalist on Twitter. All the language cited here was taken down from the various places. I also had a conversation with Pippa regarding this.* *The Great British Bake Off* (2020) had a Japanese Week, which seemed to ignore a deep Japanese culture of baking. And *MasterChef: The Professionals* (2020) allowed chef Philli Armitage-Mattin to continuously refer to ESEA food as 'dirty', instead of fast

---

* Pippa reached out to me, and we had a brief and positive phone conversation; we agreed that language is complicated and even when done unintentionally, harm can be caused, and learning and listening is key.

or street food-style dishes.* There was a constant stream of othering all while we were reading news of Filipino nurses dying at unprecedented rates and violent attacks on ESEA people in relation to Covid-19. It, quite simply, fucked me off. It is all connected, creating a narrative of less than.

The individual perpetuates upsetting narratives, but to place the blame on one person is unfair. It is an ignorance of the wider landscape fuelled by a system that doesn't have an ability to reflect, check language or sensitivities, or seem to care beyond the established norm. If we had more ESEA chefs and cooks taking up space in mainstream media, for example, maybe we wouldn't be framing the food as needing to be 'translated' or as 'alien', and there would be different palates to test 'spicy' against. If we had diversity in decision-making and power behind the cameras, we'd have different approaches to storytelling, and words like 'dirty' would be ditched before harm was done.

The food world is one that has glorified othering and made exoticism a selling point, but has also institution-alised conversations so that we are always going around and around in circles. I am quite frankly bored of the topic of cultural appropriation because it only ever stays

---

* Armitage-Mattin issued an apology on Instagram (which is now no longer live), saying that she was 'truly sorry if this has caused any offense' and explaining that she 'never called Asian food "dirty" in a derogatory manner', that she wanted to be celebratory and that she had meant the indulgence of street food and 'food that comforts you as in "going out for a dirty burger".'³

at surface level. Mainstream media is only ever interested in addressing questions like: are we allowed to cook this food? Is it appropriation to cook pasta? All too often, appropriation is conflated with authenticity. In April 2019, *Good Morning Britain* held a quintessential discussion on the cultural appropriation of food in mainstream media. Five white people discussed whether Gordon Ramsay's soon-to-be-opened restaurant Lucky Cat was culturally appropriative of Asian culture and cuisine. The criticism of the restaurant came from ESEA food journalists, critics, cooks and chefs, as well as the general public. Appropriation was discussed in relation to cooking Italian food, with chef Aldo Zilli as one of the guests, and in the vague context of authenticity. This disregarded the criticism from ESEA people, and other people of colour, which was about power and access. I wrote a critique at the time of the restaurant and situation, in *gal-dem* (a publication platforming the perspectives of people of colour from marginalised genders). Lucky Cat, I wrote in *gal-dem*, 'homogenises a whole region of the world', conflating many cultures as one, and with factually wrong reference points that fetishise Asian cultures. In response to the criticism, Ramsay said, 'Gordon Ramsay Restaurants do not discriminate based on gender, race or beliefs and we don't expect anyone else to.'[4]

Cultural appropriation is about the relationship to power and how that manifests – who gets to be successful, who gets to make money, earn kudos, thrive in the industry; who gets to the tell the story of a culture and whose culture gets to be told with nuance? It is that simple. In 2021, I wrote for CNN that Jamie Oliver is always going to appropriate because he is essentially a media empire built entirely on his own image – his power is huge, he is an institution, and his recipes cross the global culinary spectrum. The point of the piece was to address the fact he had a team of cultural experts to ensure his recipes aren't offensive: a very sensible decision for a media company to take. But if this media company, a personification of 'Jamie Oliver, the lad', is not going to give up power or space, or platform other people, and recipes are signed off under his name as 'Jamie's' (but many come from cultures not his own), then it is hard not to see it as appropriation, even if they don't call a roast chicken full of spices 'Empire Chicken'.* Jamie is still the cultural translator, when what is needed is people of a recipe's culture to be telling the story of their food heritage. East and South East Asian people need to be the storytellers, the translators, the guardians of their own stories.

Appropriation can be a messy conversation because the context is that a culture becomes a concept to sell. When we make food a business, then we are all selling it, even if it is our own culture. And food is complex because it is something we need, and it is something that is part of traditions and rituals, both in personal spaces *and* within

---

* Jamie Oliver received backlash for calling a roast chicken recipe, which had a lot of spices, 'Empire Chicken' – some of the spices used were from countries that Britain had colonised.

creating nationhood or community. And we consume it. The idea of attaching cultural identity to food, and using it as an easy (or the only) bridge for others into my culture and identity, is something I am uncomfortable with. You can't know me by eating me. Or, to paraphrase the Berlin-based Thai chef Dalad Kambhu, 'You can't cook my food, just because you have been inside me.'[5]

Jenny reminds me: 'bell hooks summarises it beautifully in her essay "Eating the Other", where she talks of how "within commodity culture, ethnicity becomes spice, seasoning that can liven up the dull dish that is mainstream white culture." '[6] This experience is what hooks calls 'fucking the Other': 'This reframes the simple us/them, native/alien binary of othering – especially where sex comes into play. Think of how we pedestalise and hand over power to people – generally men – who have "mastered" exotic cuisines, or a spiritual guru. We as humans find that mastery of the other so intoxicating. Wait... did I just describe colonialism?' These white chefs and cooks are colonialising our foods.

Even when we are aware of this system, it is hard to untangle ourselves from it. London-based Indonesian chef and food writer Rahel Stephanie says 'It is always white men who seem most entitled to appropriate marginalised cuisines, exoticise its women and romanticise its working class while they're at it. Due to wider systemic influences, subconscious self-exoticisation is still something I struggle with. When I'm presenting myself and my cultural identity with pride, I often wonder to what extent will my actions be perceived by the Eurocentric eye as exotic due to my own choices? Or to what extent are my actions and decisions subconsciously done to be perceived in a romanticised distance to the Eurocentric standard?' Within this relationship of representation, and questions about how we present ourselves in white spaces, Rahel also explains that she is constantly encountering a forcing of a familiar or maternal narrative to her cooking, something that is not the case for her. 'It's always a little jarring when the media tries to push this narrative on me. There seems to be a default vision of domesticating the South East Asian woman in some way – once again very reductive.'

There are times when responding directly to reduction and othering can work, can flip the narrative, and can even be fun. During the pandemic, Anna Chan and Georgie Ma, who runs the podcast Chinese Chippy Girl, in response to MasterChef contestant Armitage-Mattin and the word 'dirty', started the hashtag #ESEAEats on Instagram. 'It was me just saying to Georgie, look, can we do something to respond to this "dirty" labelling of our food? Why is it that anyone else is telling our stories and deciding for us what ESEA food and culture looks like?' Anna said to me. 'It was just easy to invite people to share their stories and their pictures and we thought twenty people would do it and it would be nice.' The idea took off on Instagram, with people still adding to it years later.

This is because it felt like a way to share joy, and joy feels radical when you are marginalised and angry. It was also a space were everyone could participate, including non-ESEA people, posting their experiences, travels and interpretations of food they had cooked in their home kitchens. There was no 'hand of excellence' or expertise showing the way. It was simply sharing. You could scroll the hashtag and see the array of possibility of difference, learn from people talking about their cultures. Through these moments of sharing, a community and a sense of confidence was created.

As discussed earlier in this book, the British Empire is built on the commodities of the East, and so the lens through which we view food in the UK must also take that into account. All these situations where food is the vehicle of racism are results of inequitable systems that are centuries old. They are playing on old power structures and narratives. Food makes the idea of empire tangible, the webs of it stretching across time and space. American historian Paul Freedman writes that 'everyday consumer demands affect people across the globe,' from drugs to diamonds and now oil.[7] But as he and others have stated, the desire for spices in Europe launched a trajectory of brutal colonialism and capitalism that led to enslaving people, eradicating people and cultures, and the structures we still live with today.

In 1603, James Lancaster returned to London as the commander of that first East India Company (EIC) fleet, with ships laden with pepper. By the mid 1700s, the EIC had become the ruling force in South Asia. They minted their own coins and had their own army. The eighteenth century saw the transatlantic slave trade in full force, with the British enslaving African people to work on their Caribbean sugar plantations. Britain extracted enormous revenue through extreme violence, and by the early nineteenth century, Britain had really begun to dig her claws into Asia for calico, tea and opium. By the mid-nineteenth century, the EIC was spending the equivalent of £500,000 in present day currency importing cinchon to India from South America.[8] Cinchon is a plant native to South America; it contains quinine and was used treat malaria (likely washed down with some gin and a little soda, the prequel to a G&T) so that the EIC army could continue their colonial efforts of conquering, ruling and oppressing.

In the late 1820s, the import duty on tea into London was so high that it was able to maintain 83 per cent of the Royal Navy costs.[9] By the 1830s, tea from China, then grown in Britan's colonised lands of India, had become a necessity to British life. Drunk with sugar, it was a beverage that brought together the piracy of the Empire in the East with the Empire's system of enslaving of people in the West, stimulating a workforce in Britain with empty calories to fuel the industrial revolution. Trade into China was managed through the southern city of Canton by the EIC. Steven Tsang writes, 'For much of the nineteenth century, China was the fourth most important source of imports for Britain and enjoyed a very favourable balance of bilateral trade.'[10] He notes that tea was the most important product, followed by raw silk.

But while recognising that the colonial project was an exploitative and violent one, it is also important to know that Europe didn't start a global trade network. Asia had its thriving networks long before Europe turned up. Anthropologist Michael R. Dove writes that Borneo and the Indonesian islands are linked to a wider world through a deeply historic, global commodity and trade system that dates back at least to the third century CE.[11] Pepper came from India through Sumatra to China, and those around the Sumatran ports began to grow pepper themselves to tap into the trade. The Banda Islands* in the Indonesian archipelago had nutmeg, mace and cloves as native spice that they traded too – spice that traversed all the way to Britain before Britain knew these places existed. It wasn't just those in and around the ports that were party to this trade, but also Dayak (Indigenous) people brought goods and produce from the interior jungle in Borneo to the coast to be traded.

In the 1870s, the Dutch opened up the region to private businesses, which quickly led to the corporation ownership and industrial farming we know so well today. In the 1930s, the Dutch brought in a system to Indonesia that meant selling all export crops to the

---

* The story of the Banda Islands is horrifically violent, because of the European desire to have monopoly over these spices. It is possibly one of these most upsetting histories I have read about.

colonial government at a fixed price to pay land tax. But this disrupted a carefully balanced Indigenous farming system of shifting cultivation and polyculture, which 'led to soil infertility, rice shortages, famines, peasant flight, and epidemics,' Dove writes.[12] Eradication of people and plants in pursuit of domination and ownership for money is how Europe's imperial powers imposed themselves on that vibrant trade system.

I am taking this fast romp through colonial food trade history because it shows how globally connected East and South East Asia were with the rest of the world through food, and how the trade of those foods was key to European empires. But also, this idea of Asia as a region to be exploited for the enjoyment of Europe is so ingrained in our global north understanding of the world that it is unsurprising that people and cultures of the vast Asian region are viewed as commodities *even now*.

What I am interested in now is how we shift those ideas and narratives of our foods, and therefore of ourselves. There is a need for a sort of reclamation. By shifting the focus away from white voices, who are still dictating the parameters of our food stories, we are able to centre ourselves and our histories – because food can be an entry point to discuss identity, heritage and difference; it can be very powerful. For those of us who do have a strong food culture, and whose culture can easily be expressed through food, it is helpful to find a way to connect *through* food.

But when discussing these ideas, we can fall into the

fallacy that food brings us together. I don't mean food as a fix all for racism, but rather I'm interested in seeing food as a starting point to have difficult conversations. Food can be an excuse and a conduit to inspiring discussion and bringing people *into* a room. But without interrogating that space we will continue to be stuck in shallow understandings of representation. Saying 'food brings us together' hides the power dynamics, the labour, the journeys of the people and the food. This keeps us 'in between' and 'other' as food (something that is consumed) then stands in for identity and culture.

Food allows us to ask questions, especially ones about colonialism and empire. My quick journey through history here is me answering the question 'where are you from?' Tracing history through food allows a way to explore deeper meaning, stories and histories.

But through this exchange of food and knowledge, of sharing and coming together, we can also get tripped up on stereotypes. What I love about food is its ability to make identity complicated and messy. Food works as a wonderful metaphor for identity. There is no one way to cook Malaysian chicken curry, just as there is no one way to be Malaysian. Through food, I think we can relish the mess and complexity. But first we also need to contemplate what stereotypes can do, and how we might be perpetuating them ourselves. Why do we do this?

In December 2022, Bettina Makalintal, an American journalist of Filipino heritage, wrote a piece about AI for Eater titled 'Great! AI Can Generate All the Diaspora

Writing Tropes'.* Although this is an American piece, the tropes mentioned have become universal within the global north – the 'stinky lunchbox moment' – and ChatGPT was able to construct a piece of writing that was familiar, personal and – dare I say it – at times fairly moving. And, as Makalintal writes, 'there is a tendency among writers to whittle our nuanced real-life experiences into their "most obvious and recognizable parts", with this trope-ification conveying racialised trauma that is ultimately palatable to white readers.'[13] Trying to find ways to connect can strip us of our multiplicity and nuance. It makes it easier to make us a tick box, to make us an object of otherness. We become neat and tidy in our own cliché.

I asked Makalintal about food and personal essays and she explained that she thinks people want stories that are mostly positive. 'I think this is pleasant for diasporic writers as it makes us feel as though we've briefly resolved the messiness of our feelings. I also think it's pleasant for readers – including editors – who don't share our identities because it absolves them of any role in a culture that might make people of colour feel othered. The lunchbox story is something that happens to an individual, and then they move past it, ultimately accepting their existence within a white majority culture.' This style of personal essay gets to ignore the systems, ignore feelings of shame and hatred and skip straight to finding comfort in the

---

* ChatGPT is an open AI chatbox that launched in November 2022.

system. She also explained to me that we can 'internalise a pressure to tell our stories a certain way'. Our stories are commodified for a white media landscape, through these (now) story tropes.

This isn't to say these things aren't real experiences. It's just that they aren't the only ones and some of us didn't experience them at all. Also important is the power dynamics of who gets to make profit off of a 'stinky lunchbox'. As my friend Lisa says, 'I grew up constantly hating my name, which couldn't be pronounced, being called ching chong, [white children] pulling the corner of their eyes and asking me how I can see; now the fuckers are cooking our food and opening restaurants.' Even if we find comfort by being OK with our stinky lunchboxes as we grow up, we still don't get to benefit.

Jenny sent me a list of ESEA tropes: 'constantly being told we suffer intergenerational trauma; race is the biggest barrier to equality; binary thinking and being "caught between two worlds"; allyship based on skin colour; over-attachment to food identity, to the point of taking supposed transgressions very personally.'

'I'm as much pointing out the tropes I perpetuate, but it's something I'm constantly trying to rectify through actual action,' she prefaces this list with. We all need to go through our own personal reckoning and find the language that works for us as individuals. But I wonder if in retelling these recognisable stories, we are performing trauma? Even, or especially, if they have a neat and tidy resolved ending? This isn't ignoring, but a recognition, a noting, an interrogation to living in the multiple, and not the singular. I don't want pleasantness. I want to call people fuckers. We need to find a way to be messy and complicated. Living *in* the trauma seems to me to be feeding into the whiteness, the idea of the acceptable brown/yellow/non-white face: to be saved.

I guess what I'm saying is, we can save ourselves. We don't need to be neat and tidy.

This messiness is a lived experience. Being in the UK means we are juggling multiple cultural influences and senses of belonging. We have mixed ethnicities and/or are part of multiple cultures,* food is a great tool for learning about the specificities of our heritages. John Chantarasak, chef and co-owner of AngloThai restaurant in London, was born in Liverpool, and has lived in Pwllmeyric in Wales, New York, Bangkok and now in London. He told me how his father came to the UK from Thailand for secondary school. It took John some time to understand his Thai background, although as children he and his siblings did visit for holidays. It was through food that he chose to engage with his heritage, moving to Bangkok to study cooking and learn the language.

In contrast with the frustration I felt at his appearance on *Great British Menu*, John explains to me: 'Most people

---

* This is not just a mixed-race experience, for example those who are British-born and whose parents are both of ESEA heritage may also feel they are part of two or more cultures.

[in the UK] have only really had interaction with some of the more commonly found dishes outside of Thailand, like pad thai, green curry and fish cakes. I've learnt to think about my audience when I cook now and do take spice into consideration.' This doesn't mean a dumbing down or any sort of compromise – John cooks some very hot dishes. It is instead an acknowledgment of multiple interpretations and a creative and open approach to cooking. 'Like any food culture, there's so much to discover with the cuisine. It's not uncommon that people can't handle the spice level of some dishes. Even when I travel in specific areas of Thailand, I find the heat of the food a little challenging. I have some savage meal memories from southern Thailand in particular!' John says. His approach is to be incredibly transparent about his dual heritage and his cooking has found a home in that intersection.

Rahel feels that part of her job is about trying to tell the story of diversity. Her heritage is of the ethnic Batak tribe, one of more than 200 ethnicities in Indonesia. This is also about dispelling misconceptions: 'The *Jakarta Post* counted 252 unique sate varieties in Indonesia – many of which have nothing to do with peanuts whatsoever. And then there's the "tempe" problem. Over the years, I observed the growing popularity and Westernisation of it as a "superfood" and meat substitute. Its humble roots are far from this. It was eaten by those who were not able to afford meat as a cheap source of protein, and its creation from a traditional zero-waste culture was more from necessity than choice. Quite a contrast to its current mainstream incarnation.'[14] This is also a reminder that what is 'exotic' in one location is a staple in another.

Like John and Rahel, Malaysian food is how I get to address my sense of multiple-ness. In Sarawak alone there are over twenty-eight Indigenous peoples, plus Chinese of various heritage, various South Asian communities, Malay and Europeans and, of course, a lot of mixed-race people. Malaysia is country with thirteen states and three federal territories. It has a monarch as head of state – there are nine royal families and the title of King gets rotated on a five-year term. There are many religions and traditions, not to mention languages spoken throughout the country. Although it is an Islamic state there are national holidays for Gawai and Chinese New Year, as well as Hari Raya. This is not to say that Malaysia is some utopian paradise though. There are many hierarchies in place, including racism, classism, so much homophobia, misogyny . . . but through food there is a beginning idea of difference.

Vera Chok says, 'Malaysian to me means being obsessed with food. I used to eat every four hours – breakfast, mid-morning snack, lunch, tea, dinner, supper and then mamak o'clock. I joke that you can tell time by when I get hungry, in four-hour increments. Malaysian for me also means multicultural and multilingual. It means: having a unique perspective of East and West; being South East Asian; having a healthy fear of natural and ancestral spirits that reside in the unknown spaces of jungle and waters. I'm aspirational in a way that comes from being from a new country.'

But being Malaysian in the UK means all these nuances and differences get simplified, and we are represented through only a handful of dishes: roti canai, beef rendang, nasi lemak, nasi goreng, some samba and now laksa. Mandy Yin,* my friend and the owner of Sambal Shiok restaurant, said to me once that her pet hate was how often food journalists call Malaysian restaurants 'Malay'! It had not occurred to me that people didn't understand the difference between 'Malay' and being 'Malaysian', but now I see it everywhere. Malay refers to a group of people and is both an ethnicity and a cultural group. A large part of South East Asia – Singapore, Malaysia, Indonesia, Philippines – was referred to as the Malay region, due to the history of Islamic kingdoms. Malay people are predominantly Muslim, and their cultural traditions are varied depending on individual families or where they are from. For example, in East Malaysia, a number of Dayak groups converted to Islam and are bureaucratically identified as Malay. Malaysian food is naturally influenced from all the countries' cultures. Not all Malaysian food is Malay, not all Malay food is Malaysian.

In the UK, we can see the diversity of Malaysian-ness, and South East Asian-ness through food but we have to be deliberate and look for the nuances. Cook and

---

* Mandy's book, *Sambal Shiok: The Malaysian Cookbook*, is an excellent example of showing how diverse Malaysia is through food and flavour, and connecting migration to the evolving food traditions.

197

table stylist Kirthanaa Naidu uses food to explore her Malaysian identity in the UK. Known for her pandan cheesecakes, she is of South Asian heritage but is very much a Malaysian living in London. Chinese Malaysian Mandy's Sambal Shiok is a laksa bar pulling on Peranakan influences in her laksa. Roti King's founders are of South Asian heritage, making the Tamil-influenced Malaysian roti canai; Normah's restaurant is run by Malay Malaysian Normah Adb Hamin who cooks traditional halal Malay foods – from beef rendang to laksa.

But it isn't just Malaysia, or South East Asia, that have histories that complicate the ESEA identity and narrative. Doug Hing is a Londoner with Chinese Caribbean heritage. He told me about discovering a place in Hong Kong that cooks a curry *just* the way that his grandmother did, only to find out that the chef had learnt that recipe from a Bangladeshi cook; and how there is an amazing Caribbean roti restaurant in South London run by a Guyanese couple – one of whom is Debbie, who is of Chinese heritage.

Doug's father believes his grandparents arrived in Guyana around 1890, and that his mother's grandparents arrived in Trinidad in the 1850s. 'This is a long time to be away from your "ethnic" home,' he says. His parents migrated to Britain and met at a 'Tea Dance', an event that included partner dancing; his mother came to study to be a doctor and ended up in nursing, while his father held administrative roles, including for British Airways. Doug explains that he doesn't 'feel' particularly Chinese:

CHINESE AND ANY OTHER ASIAN

his father doesn't cook Chinese food, he cooks Caribbean food. His older brother and sister went to Chinese school in London, and he was sent to kung fu lessons, but his identity is predominantly a Caribbean identity, which is a connection made through food. 'My dad had friends who worked in market stalls in Brixton; I had an uncle, a Jamaican Chinese man – the strongest Jamaican accent, coming from a Chinese man – who had a Jamaican Chinese takeaway shop. My first job was working on a market stall in Balham. I grew up with Black [Caribbean] people and feel more comfortable with that [British Caribbean] community.' When thinking about ESEA communities, I think about how expansive we can be to include these multiplicities. It is through food, and our relationships with the different foods we eat, that I think we will find that way into being inclusive. The Jamaican Chinese takeaway shop is a British heritage, it is a Chinese heritage, it is a Caribbean heritage.

Indeed, British Chinese takeaway food has become its own identity and staple within the cultural landscape of the country. Due to immigration from the then British-ruled Hong Kong, Cantonese people were the predominant migrants, setting up early takeaways and restaurants that catered to the local Western palate and incorporated other colonial migrant influences. The dishes that have come out of this blending – chips and curry sauce, prawn toast, sweet and sour chicken – are all uniquely British. They have differences across regions, from shop to shop, and have authenticity in their own right. Jenny suggests we think of British Chinese cooking as a regional Chinese cuisine. And Chinese food in Britain will also shift as new migrants come, and as the next generation of British Chinese chefs and cooks push and experiment with their own culinary journeys.

It is this complexity and intersection of different identities that many people within the ESEA communities are trying to explore through food, and it has become important to explore that within our own communities. Jenny runs the platform Celestial Peach, which started as a way for her to examine her connection with identity, predominantly through food. It has developed beyond that to include a space for mostly ESEA people to meet both online via her website and her Instagram page, and in-person. Although she wouldn't ever want to tell anyone they couldn't come to an event, she is careful about the way she words some of her invitations, saying 'my events are "weighted" towards people of ESEA heritage' and leaving that for people to interpret as they wish.

'The exclusive–inclusivity dichotomy is one that I must navigate delicately, especially with the community events that I curate, which run on a "by and for" ethos. I guess that is the true meaning of "grassroots". I'm most passionate about facilitating non-transactional exchange – of food, ideas, conversation, experiences – rather than finding a way to commodify our cultural practices,' Jenny explains. 'Every time we end one of those in-person events, people tell me afterwards how much it lifted their spirits. I believe it's not just the good food that we're sharing, but that we all feel seen and validated. It's healing on a micro level. And that healing can only happen when it's a space full of people who look like you, because living as lifelong diaspora in white dominant spaces does warp your sense of self. That's why exclusivity is important.'

At the back of my dad and stepmother's house in Kuching is an open fireplace, a barbeque spot, where we gather with family and friends. My stepmother has planted a number of plants along the side – pandan, turmeric, cangkok manis (leaf greens), kantan (torched ginger), bungkang* – and the space has become more and more organised over the years to the point that my dad put up a sign on the tree above his chair that said: 'dad's shed'.

It is a space I think of often. When the summer sun shines in London, I try and recreate it in my garden. An open-fire barbeque, friends and family. Most years I host Gawai, our harvest festival, akin to New Year celebrations. It is a party-like ceremony of bringing people together with the excuse of eating, and it feels like what being Iban means to me. I add tuak† and, of course, durian to the mix. I am laying claim to the idea that my right to eat and drink – to party – is a cultural heritage.

---

* Leaves used in the Iban dish manok pansoh: chicken cooked in bamboo, over fire.
† This is a drink made from rice, brewed more like beer but with an ABV more akin to wine. It is specifically Dayak, but the Iban versions are generally more potent!

I want to approach ideas of identity and navigating identity outside of a Western framework of them/us dichotomy, and to look outside of binary notions to explore complex narratives. Through Sarawakian and Malaysian food, I have grown up seeing how cultures and traditions have influenced each other, how migration has created new traditions and stories, but also how it is possible to have clear and distinct identities. The fact that every region, and every town, has their own version of laksa, and yet laksa is a 'Malaysian' dish, sums it up for me – specific, multiple, general. Britain is a similar place, a space of multiples, of complex heritage that we should be relishing.

We can be un-tick-box-able.

We *must* be un-tick-box-able.

Conclusion

Hidden Faces

There is a Malaysian restaurant just behind Euston station in London. It is a tiny basement spot that has become a cultural hit for Londoners and always has a queue outside. One very cold, but beautifully sunny, winter afternoon, I stood in the queue with my friend Lucinda Newns and her husband, Doug Hing. It was the right level of cold to build up an appetite.

The restaurant is Roti King and they specialise in roti canai, which is a flaky flatbread served with a small bowl of dal or curry to dip the roti in. It is a dish I think of as quintessentially Malaysian, but also has a home in a number of South East Asian countries – particularly Singapore, Indonesia, Brunei and Thailand. As with the story of many foods, it is hard to place its exact origins, but it is a dish of Indian influences and likely came from Tamil labourers during the British control of Malaya (West Malaysia). I know it as a breakfast dish, and I always have it kosong (plain) with chicken curry.

As we stood out in the cold waiting for a table, stamping our feet to keep them warm, I discussed with Lucinda (an Irish American academic teaching and researching post-colonial literature with a particular focus on the Caribbean) and Doug (a Londoner of Chinese Caribbean heritage) about the difficulties with this book of tracing histories and finding information. Lucinda told me about how she's always been intrigued by the images of the arrival of HMT *Empire Windrush*, seen through the footage created by British Pathé – on YouTube 'Reporter Meets (1948)'[1] – where you can see East Asian male faces on the ship among the Black Caribbean men,* and of a photo she's seen many times which featured some members of the Bloomsbury Group and one woman who looks East Asian who is never named.† Over lunch, Doug tells me about his family's migration story, from China to Guyana to London. We discuss the idea of hidden faces in history, the lost stories.

The process of writing this book has been about trying to tell some of these stories, to purposefully make faces un-hidden, to record, to re-record. This book's aim is to give a context to the world we live in today. Although

---

* Also striking in this clip is a calypso singer, Lord Kitchener, who sings a song about London, and 'coming home' to London and his 'mother country'.

† 'It was taken at the BBC studios during a production of the radio show *Caribbean Voices*, which was pioneering Caribbean literature at the time. It features Una Marson (centre, who led the show at the time), Mulk Raj Anand, George Orwell and T.S. Eliot – Marson and Eliot were associated with the Bloomsbury Group, though not exactly members. The East Asian-looking woman standing behind them is never named in any of the captions I've seen,' Lucinda explains to me.

I've delved into the past, I've wanted to really give space to voices of today that are shaping our future. This work hasn't been about a 'discovery' of people, stories or histories but feels more like a witnessing and a re-witnessing. So many of the specific stories I heard from people haven't made it in, but everyone I spoke to is in the pages of this book in some way. Through them, I have been able to add nuance and understanding. I hope that the array of people featured here only makes us eager to listen to, and listen out for, the many stories – to seek those stories out. There are a multitude of intricate and complex lives, cultures and histories within the communities of people from East and South East Asian heritages.

Through researching this book, I have found so many people doing amazing work that complicates the narrative around ESEA identity in the UK. As someone who uses food and drink to research culture and history, and whose journalistic work is predominantly on food and drink, I've personally noticed that Filipino food has become a lot more known in recent years, which I find deeply exciting. This is not some idea of a 'trend' but because incredible Filipino chefs and cooks – such as Budgie Montoya, Mark Corbyn, Mary San Pablo and Mae Williams to name a few – are not only championing their food, but also talking and writing about it with context of the colonial history with Spain and America alongside ideas of authenticity, plus giving space to Indigenous histories across the archipelago. And when I interviewed British Chinese cooks and chefs about what they were excited about regarding the future of British Chinese food, they all spoke about regional specificity becoming more widely understood. With that comes a space for innovation, as well as a desire to know more with nuance.

Georgina has written a lot about more recent histories of working-class ESEA people, in particularly Vietnamese communities. Her ability to weave in personal memory along with telling the stories of others allows vivid pictures to be painted. In the summer of 2022, she wrote an article for *Huck* magazine that looked at the Hackney 'Pho Mile', a strip in the East London borough that has become a community hub for Vietnamese people. Most of these restaurants grew from newly arrived refugees from the late 1970s onwards and Georgina tells the stories of the individuals, ensuring that readers understand the many faces that make up this now historic and culturally important part of London's culinary landscape.[2] The Museum of Home in Hackney ran a series of artist residencies in 2023 that focused on 'activating Vietnamese archives through a contemporary lens'. It was an in-depth exploration that involved workshops for the public to participate in and a range of different artists. Some of the workshops were only for those of ESEA background and gave priority to those of Vietnamese heritage. These are acts creating space and giving power to those who these histories belong to.

Madévi explained to me that the lack of ties and history with Cambodia means that people struggle to place her in the UK. 'I find that people in the UK are far less likely to know or guess where I'm from. I think

I'm quite confusing to the average British person: I don't have a French accent, I don't look or sound like what they expect from an Asian person – whatever that means! – and I'm neither a refugee nor an economic migrant.' But, for Madévi, this is fun. 'I quite enjoy letting people stew in their preconceptions when they ask me about my origins: it forces them into some degree of self-awareness about their own prejudices.' It is with this sense of fun that she continues to explore her identity, and it is this humour I see often in ESEA people when talking about identity and tackling difficult topics. How I 'met' Madévi was because she posted a Twitter thread during the 2022 summer heatwave in the UK: 'Hi, bonafide half-Cambodian here. I know a thing or two about keeping cool in hot weather. Thought I'd share my ancestral wisdom with you.'[3]

It started with basic facts, find shade, do nothing. Then swiftly into 'Criticise that niece of yours who is ungrateful and also not as thin as she used to be,' and 'Wear a sarong. It does not matter if you're a man or a woman, gotta keep that downstairs breeze going,' to 'Eat the fruit your nephew brought you as a mark of his respect. He's much better behaved than his sister but he could do with putting a bit of weight on, he's all skin and bones he will never find a wife looking like that.' It was hysterical, poking fun at earnest Twitter threads and South East Asian stereotypes; it was an in-joke for South East Asians. It was for us. And I hope that this book has been a place for fun too, a place to play around and re-see our identities; and for those outside of ESEA identities to understand this as well.

I have avoided addressing the word 'authentic' in this book because it hampers the way we look at things. We can get so tangled up in this word. But, to add some John Wick-style chaos in at the eleventh hour, I want to talk about it here. Authenticity gets confused with traditions and rituals. It also gets caught up with the idea of 'the' truth instead of being seen as 'a' truth. Authenticity is used as a form of policing. My friend Lisa has explained to me that as well as being inspired by the success of small ESEA food businesses: 'it is also upsetting. I see the hate clubs from Asians; pulling people down when it's not deemed "authentic".' And that policing is done externally. We are forced to tell stories that outsiders deem as authentic, hence the never-ending lunchbox stories, the need to live in trauma. We tie ourselves up in knots to prove our pain is *authentic*, so as to be believed, to be worthy of care and attention. Non-ESEA people claim authenticity over our food, our stories, our culture so that they can justify appropriating them, but do not acknowledge whose authenticity it is, whose voice and knowledge they are referencing, because this de-centres them. The search for and struggle over authenticity can strip us of joy, which gives us the ability to thrive. What is authenticity but a perceived notion? We are all living an authentic life already because that is the life we know. Our individual personal, family, community lens on the world is an authentic one. The journey your story has taken to be here is part of that authentic story – in all its multiplicity, its joy, its trauma, its silliness and its pain.

'The social and environmental changes which have caused the disappearance of some Iban rituals are the very factors which have generated the emergence of new ones,' my father wrote in his PhD conclusion.[4] To me, this sums up the way we live in a diasporic space. We are creating rituals and home, creating new ones, and folding in old ones. Our idea of tradition and authenticity moves and evolves as our identities grow and change. In deepening our roots in this country, we become dynamic and full of motion. We gather, we disperse, and return to each other again.

After our lunch at Roti King, Lucinda, Doug and I went to the British Library to see an exhibition on British Chinese people. We saw an exhibit about the Chinese writer Ling Shuhua, who spent four decades of her life in London and was linked to the Bloomsbury Group, and wonder if that might be the unnamed woman Lucinda was talking about in the famous photo.

The exhibition detailed stories of Chinese people and communities in the UK dating back centuries, showing the long history of East Asian people in Britain. It showed a strong link between Britain and Hong Kong and the New Territories, so an understanding of a British Chinese identity that comes from those ties was demonstrated. I personally would have liked the exhibition to have been more specific, to really show the colonial context, to demonstrate the complex difference even within this very specific context. Or to be much more broad and to give a large showing of the myriad of British Chinese stories.

At the end of the exhibition, Doug turned to me and said: 'I don't see me represented in any way here.' The exhibition begged the question: what is Chinese?

The enormous institute of the British Library, both in size of building and in reputation, had relegated the telling of a deeply diverse, culturally rich and varied history of British people of Chinese heritage to a small basement room. There was no room for real nuance, for specificity or large sweeping vistas of what British Chinese can and could mean. To me, it said a lot about our place in the cultural landscape of Britain, but I also realised that my disappointment was because there are so few spaces for these stories to be told that I wanted this one opportunity to do so much, which it could never do. The work that went into the exhibition was incredible, and my only conclusion is that we just need more of these spaces, we need to take up more room, more rooms, in many, many different types of spaces – institutional and community.

Despite the work that so many of us have done, over months, years, decades and centuries, there is still so much to do, so many ways to shift and change how people from East and South East Asian heritages – in all that can mean – are seen, valued, loved, cherished and respected.

In the introduction, I said this book was an invitation for others to tell their stories. This book is also an invitation to individuals and institutions to bring more of our stories into centre from the periphery. Because we refuse to be hidden, to be a tick box lost in vagueness. We don't just want to be at the party, we are the party.

Reading List

There are so many books I have read over the years that have led me to think and write critically about race, gender, identity and colonialism, and not all of them have made it into this book as quoted texts. Therefore, I wanted to put together a short reading list of some (favourite) books that have either been background research to this book or helped establish my thinking. I would, of course, recommend all the books and articles I have quoted throughout!

America's Lost Chinese: The Rise and Fall of a Migrant Family Dream by Hugo Wong. London: C. Hurst & Co Publishers Ltd., 2023.

Black Looks: Race and Representation, Second Edition by bell hooks. London: Routledge, 2014.

Borderlands / La Frontera: The New Mestiza, Fourth Edition by Gloria Anzaldúa. San Francisco: Aunt Lute Books, 2012.

Culture and Imperialism by Edward W. Said. London: Vintage, 1994.

Doreen Massey: Selected Political Writings by Doreen Massey, ed. David Featherstone and Diarmaid Kelliher. London: Lawrence and Wishart, 2022.

Natives: Race and Class in the Ruins of Empire by Akala. London: Two Roads, 2018.

Sweetness and Power: The Place of Sugar in Modern History by Sidney W. Mintz. London: Penguin, 1968.

The Hungry Empire: How Britain's Quest for Food Shaped the Modern World by Lizzie Collingham. London: Vintage, 2018.

Woman, Native, Other: Writing Postcoloniality and Feminism by Trinh T. Minh-ha. Indiana: Indiana University Press, 1989.

Your Silence Will Not Protect You: Essays and Poems by Audre Lorde. London: Silver Press, 2017.

Endnotes

Introduction: Borders and Beginnings

1   Said, E.W. cited in Frayling, C. *The Yellow Peril: Dr Fu Manchu & The Rise of Chinaphobia*. London: Thames and Hudson Ltd, 2014.

2   Frayling, C. *The Yellow Peril: Dr Fu Manchu & The Rise of Chinaphobia*. London: Thames and Hudson Ltd, 2014.

3   Hall, S. 'Black Chronicles II' exhibition, London: Rivington Place, 2014. Cited in O'Hagan, S. 'The black Victorians: astonishing portraits unseen for 120 years'. *Guardian*, 2014. Available at: https://www.theguardian.com/artanddesign/2014/sep/15/black-chronicles-ii-victorians-photography-exhibition-rivington-place [accessed 11 July 2024].

Chapter 1: Language

1   Said, E.W. *Orientalism*. London: Penguin Books, 2003.

2   Evans, N. and Evans, N. *The Mixed-Race Experience: Reflections and Revelations on Multicultural Identity*. London: Vintage, 2023.

3   Office for National Statistics. 'The changing picture of long-term international migration, England and Wales: Census 2021'. Gov.uk, 2023. Available at: https://www.ons.gov.uk/peoplepopulationandcommunity/populationandmigration/internationalmigration/articles/thechangingpictureoflongterm

internationalmigrationenglandandwales/census2021 [accessed 10 July 2024].

4 Office for National Statistics. 'Analysis of social characteristics of international migrants living in England and Wales: Census 2021'. Gov.uk, 2023. Available at: https://www.ons.gov.uk/peoplepopulationandcommunity/populationandmigration/internationalmigration/articles/analysisofsocialcharacteristics ofinternationalmigrantslivinginenglandandwales/census2021 [accessed 10 July 2024].

5 Office for National Statistics. 'Ethnic group, England and Wales: Census 2021'. Gov.uk, 2022. Available at: https://www.ons.gov.uk/peoplepopulationandcommunity/culturalidentity/ethnicity/bulletins/ethnicgroupenglandandwales/census2021 [accessed 10 June 2024].

6 Ibid.

7 Office for National Statistics. 'Ethnic group (detailed): Census 2021'. Gov.uk, 2023. Available at: https://www.ons.gov.uk/datasets/TS022/editions/2021/versions/2 [accessed 10 June 2024].

8 Office for National Statistics. 'Why have Black and South Asian people been hit hardest by COVID-19?'. Gov.uk, 2020. Available at: https://www.ons.gov.uk/peoplepopulationandcommunity/healthandsocialcare/conditionsanddiseases/articles/whyhave bla ckandsouthasianpeoplebeenhithardestbycovid19/2020-12-14 [accessed 10 July 2024].

9 El-Enany, N. *Bordering Britain: Law, Race and Empire*. Manchester: Manchester University Press, 2020.

10 Lee, G.B. '#chinesevirus: The Long Racism that Lurks Behind COVID-19'. *Postcolonial Politics*, 2021. Available at: https://postcolonialpolitics.org/chinesevirus-racism-behind-covid-19/ [accessed 21 May 2024].

11 Yeh, D. 'Becoming British East Asian and Southeast Asian: Anti-racism, Chineseness, and Political Love in the Cultural and

Creative Industries'. *British Journal of Chinese Studies*, 11, 53–70, 2021. https://doi.org/10.51661/bjocs.v11i0.131.

12 Jin, M. 'Strangers in a Hostile Landscape' in Cobham, R. and Collins, M. (eds.) *Watchers and Seekers: Original Anthology of Creative Writing by Black Women Living in Britain*. London: The Women's Press Ltd, 1987.

13 Lee, G.B. '#chinesevirus: The Long Racism that Lurks Behind COVID-19', 2021. (n.10).

14 Yeh, D. 'Becoming British East Asian and Southeast Asian', 2021. (n.11).

15 Hughes, E. 'Award-Winning Chocolatier Equates Domestic Abuse with a Southeast Asian Delicacy'. *Eater*, 2019. Available at: https://london.eater.com/2019/2/14/18224846/paul-a-young-chocolate-domestic-abuse-awareness-durian-fruit-london [accessed 21 May 2014].

16 Lebo, K. *The Book of Difficult Fruit: Arguments for the Tart, Tender and Unruly*. London: Picador, 2021.

17 Khor, S. 'Award-Winning UK Chocolatier Faces Backlash For Using Durian To Represent Domestic Abuse'. SAYS [online], 18 February 2019. Available at: https://says.com/my/lifestyle/uk-chocolatier-under-fire-for-using-durian-to-symbolise-domestic-abuse [accessed 25 July 2024].

18 Massey, D. *For Space*. London: SAGE Publications, 2005.

19 Masing, A.S. 'I walk, I run, I dance into the beyond' in *East Side Voices: Essay Celebrating East and Southeast Asian Identity in Britain*, Lee. H. (ed.) London: Sceptre, 2022.

20 Masing, J.J. 'The Coming of the Gods: A Study of an Invocatory Chant (Timang Gawai Amat) of the Iban of the Baleh River Region of Sarawak'. Canberra: Australian National University, 1981.

Chapter 2: Empire and Migration

1 Geoghegan, P. 'Brexit: The UK's rage against dying of colonial light'. Al Jazeera, Aljazeera.com, 2016. Available at: https://www.aljazeera.com/opinions/2016/6/20/brexit-the-uks-rage-against-dying-of-colonial-light [accessed 21 May 2024].

2 Hirsch, A. 'This is a Britain that has lost its Queen – and the luxury of denial about its past'. *Guardian*, 2022. Available at: https://www.theguardian.com/commentisfree/2022/sep/13/queen-reign-death-elizabeth-ii-uk-minorities-british-empire [accessed 21 May 2024].

3 Koegler, C., Malreddy, P.K., Tronicke, M. 'The colonial remains of Brexit: Empire nostalgia and narcissistic nationalism'. *Journal of Postcolonial Writing*, 56(5), 585–592, 2020. https://doi.org/10.1080/17449855.2020.1818440.

4 von Tunzelmann, A. *Indian Summer: The Secret History of the End of an Empire*. London: Pocket Books, 2017.

5 Freedman, P. *Out of the East: Spices and the Medieval Imagination*. New Haven, Connecticut: Yale University Press, 2009.

6 von Tunzelmann, A. *Indian Summer*, 2017. (no.4).

7 Pomfret, D.M. *Youth and Empire: Trans-Colonial Children in British and French Asia*. Stanford: Stanford University Press, 2015.

8 Tsang, S. *A Modern History of Hong Kong: 1841–1997*. London: Bloomsbury Academic, 2019.

9 Patel, I.S. *We're Here Because You Were There: Immigration and the End of Empire*. London: Verso Books, 2021.

10 Mintz, S.W. 'Introduction' in Look Lai, W. *Indentured Labor, Caribbean Sugar: Chinese and Indian Migrants to the British West Indies, 1838–1918, Revised Edition*. Baltimore: John Hopkins University Press, 2004.

11 Patel, I.S. *We're Here Because You Were There*, 2021. (no.9).

12 Look Lai, W. *The Chinese in the West Indies 1806–1995: A*

Documentary History. Mona, Saint Andrew Parish, Jamaica: University of the West Indies Press, 2000.

13 Look Lai, W. *Indentured Labor, Caribbean Sugar: Chinese and Indian Migrants to the British West Indies, 1838–1918, Revised Edition*. Baltimore: John Hopkins University Press, 2004.

14 Hancox, D. 'The secret deportations: how Britain betrayed the Chinese men who served the country in the war'. *Guardian*, 2021. Available at: https://www.theguardian.com/news/2021/may/25/chinese-merchant-seamen-liverpool-deportations [accessed 9 July 2024].

15 Shang, A. cited in Hsiao, Y. in ' "Take-Away" My Childhood: The Second-Generation British Chinese in the Catering Trade'. *Journal of Ethnic and Cultural Studies*, 7(3):34, 2020. https://doi.org/10.29333/ejecs/341.

16 Watson, J.L. *Emigration and the Chinese Lineage: The 'Mans' in Hong Kong and London*. Berkeley: University of California Press, 1975.

17 El-Enany, N. *Bordering Britain: Law, Race and Empire*. Manchester: Manchester University Press, 2020. (p.81).

18 Patel, I.S. *We're Here Because You Were There*, 2021. p.62. (no.9).

19 El-Enany, N. *Bordering Britain*, 2020. (n.17).

20 Davidson, H. ' "Hong Kong 47 trial": 14 activists found guilty of conspiracy to commit subversion'. *Guardian*, 30 May 2024. Available at: https://www.theguardian.com/world/article/2024/may/30/hong-kong-47-trial-verdict-pro-democracy-campaigners-national-security [accessed 17 July 2024].

21 Patel, P. 'Hong Kong British National (Overseas) Visa and Suspension of Extradition Treaty with Hong Kong'. UK Parliament [online], 2020. Available at: https://questions-statements.parliament.uk/written-statements/detail/2020-07-22/HCWS421 [accessed 9 July 2024].

22 UK Home Office policy paper. 'New Plan for Immigration: legal migration and border control strategy statement 2021 (accessible

web version)'. Gov.uk, 24 May 2021. Available at: https://www.
gov.uk/government/publications/new-plan-for-immigration-legal-
migration-and-border-control/new-plan-for-immigration-legal-
migration-and-border-control-strategy-statement-accessible-web-
version [accessed 17 July 2024].

23 Taylor, B. ' "Our Most Foreign Refugees": Refugees from Vietnam
in Britain' in Taylor, B., Akoka, K., Berlinghoff, M., Havkin, S.
(eds.) *When Boat People were Resettled, 1975–1983: A Comparative
History of European and Israeli Responses to the South-East Asian
Refugee Crisis.* London: Palgrave Macmillan, 2021.

24 El-Enany, N. *Bordering Britain*, 2020. (n.17).

25 Patel, I.S. *We're Here Because You Were There*, 2021. (n.9).

Chapter 3: Violence

1 Schumann, S. and Moore, Y. 'The COVID-19 Outbreak as
a Trigger Event for Sinophobic Hate Crimes in the United
Kingdom'. *The British Journal of Criminology*, 63(2), 367–383,
2023. https://doi.org/10.1093/bjc/azac015.

2 Public Health England. 'Disparities in the risk and outcomes
of COVID-19'. Gov.uk, 2020. Available at: https://assets.
publishing.service.gov.uk/media/5f328354d3bf7f1b12a7023a/
Disparities_in_the_risk_and_outcomes_of_COVID_August_
2020_update.pdf [accessed 21 May 2024].

3 Ford, M. 'High death rates among Filipino nurses in UK now
on global radar'. *Nursing Times*, 2020. Available at: https://www.
nursingtimes.net/news/coronavirus/high-death-rates-among-
filipino-nurses-in-uk-now-on-global-radar-05-06-2020/ [accessed
21 May 2024].

4 Li, J. @dumplingshack post on Instagram.com, 29 March 2021.

5 Commission for Countering Extremism. 'COVID-19: How
hateful extremists are exploiting the pandemic'. Gov.uk, July
2020. Available at: https://assets.publishing.service.gov.uk/

media/5f2952308fa8f57acebf6794/CCE_Briefing_Note_001.pdf [accessed 17 July 2024].

6 besea.n. 'Face of the virus: Problematic over-representation of East and South East Asian faces in news coverage of the COVID-19 pandemic'. besea.n, 2021. Available at: https://static1.squarespace. com/static/5f369d95ba72601ce27f00bf/t/617c2057dd067861917b8 4fa/1635524827909/Face+of+the+virus-besea.n-2021.pdf [accessed 17 July 2024].

7 Barabantseva, E. 'Seeing beyond the ethnic enclave: the time/ space of Manchester's Chinatown'. *Identities*, 23(1), 99–115, 2015. https://doi.org/10.1080/1070289X.2015.1016522.

8 Hui, A. 'The Stark Reality of Racism for East and South East Asian Women in the UK'. *Refinery29*, 2021. Available at: https://www.refinery29.com/en-gb/asian-women-hate-racism-uk [accessed 5 June 2024].

9 Hui, A. *Takeaway: Stories from a childhood behind the counter.* London: Trapeze, 2022.

10 Johnson, N. N., and Johnson, T. L. 'Microaggressions: An Introduction' in Thomas, U. (ed.). *Navigating Micro-Aggressions Toward Women in Higher Education* (pp. 1–22). IGI Global, 2019. https://doi.org/10.4018/978-1-5225-5942-9.ch001.

11 Shih, S., Tsai, C. and Bernards, B. (eds.) *Sinophone Studies: A Critical Reader.* New York City: Columbia University Press, 2013.

12 Ibid.

13 Tan, C., Storey, C. and Zimmerman, J. (eds.) *Chinese Overseas: Migration, Research and Documentation.* Hong Kong: The Chinese University Press, 2008.

14 Sunak, R. @RishiSunak post on X.com (formerly Twitter.com), 25 July 2022.

15 Mordaunt, P. @PennyMordaunt post on X.com (formerly Twitter. com), 19 July 2022.

16 Willcox, E. 'Trafficking gangs involved in Morecambe Bay cockling tragedy "untouchable" 20 years on'. ITV Granada,

6 February 2024. Available at: https://www.itv.com/news/
granada/2024-02-05/chinese-triad-gangs-involved-in-morecambe-
bay-tragedy-untouchable [accessed 18 July 2024].

17 Kagan, C. *et al.* 'Experiences of forced labour among Chinese
migrant workers'. *International Journal of Work Organisation and
Emotion*, 5(3):261–280, 2013. https://doi.org/10.1504/IJWOE.2013.
055905.

18 Archer, I. and Clements, M. 'International Migrants Day: Global
Analysis 2023'. Business & Human Rights Resource Centre,
December 2023. Available at: https://www.business-humanrights.
org/en/from-us/briefings/migrant-workers-2023/migrant-workers-
rights-global-analysis-2023/ [accessed 18 July 2024].

19 Unseen. 'Annual assessment 2023'. Unseen, 2023. Available at:
https://www.unseenuk.org/wp-content/uploads/2024/05/Unseen-
Helpline-Annual-Assessment_2023.pdf [accessed 18 July 2024].

20 Business & Human Rights Resource Centre. 'UK: Modern
slavery helpline, Unseen, sees significant rise in cases of abuse
and forced labour in the care sector'. Business & Human Rights
Resource Centre, 22 October 2023. Available at: https://www.
business-humanrights.org/en/latest-news/uk-modern-slavery-
helpline-unseen-sees-significant-rise-in-cases-of-abuse-forced-
labour-in-the-care-sector/ [accessed 18 July 2024].

21 Fraser, C. 'Asian Care Worker Abuse in the Global North: A
Call for Greater Corporate Accountability'. *The Diplomat*, 27
February 2024. Available at: https://thediplomat.com/2024/02/
asian-care-worker-abuse-in-the-global-north-a-call-for-greater-
corporate-accountability/ [accessed 18 July 2024].

22 UNSION. 'Migrant care staff in UK "exploited and harassed"
by employers, says UNISON'. UNISON, 10 July 2023. Available
at: https://www.unison.org.uk/news/press-release/2023/07/
migrant-care-staff-in-uk-exploited-and-harassed-by-employers-
says-unison/ [accessed 28 July 2024].

23 Thiemann, I. *et al.* 'UK agriculture and care visas: worker

exploitation and obstacles to redress'. Modern Slavery and Human Rights Policy and Evidence Centre (online), 11 March 2024. https://www.modernslaverypec.org/resources/uk-agriculture-care-visas-vulnerability-exploitation [accessed 18 July 2024].

24 Adamson, S. *et al.* *Hidden from public view? Racism against the UK Chinese population.* London: The Monitoring Group, 2009.

25 Diab, R. and Godbee, B. 'Do We Really Understand Microaggressions?'. *Ms. Magazine*, 2022. Available at https://msmagazine.com/2022/03/04/microaggressions/ [accessed 21 May 2024].

Chapter 4: Gender

1 Bellebono, J. 'Ladyboy' in *East Side Voices: Essay Celebrating East and Southeast Asian Identity in Britain*, Lee. H. (ed.) London: Sceptre, 2022.

2 Masing, J.J. 'The Coming of the Gods: A Study of an Invocatory Chant (Timang Gawai Amat) of the Iban of the Baleh River Region of Sarawak'. Canberra: Australian National University, 1981.

3 Bechdel, A. quoted in Anderson, H. 'Interview: Alison Bechdel: 'The Bechdel Test was a joke . . . I didn't intend for it to become a real gauge'. *Guardian*, 2023. Available at: https://www.theguardian.com/books/2023/jul/02/alison-bechdel-test-dykes-to-watch-out-for-cartoonist-interview [accessed 5 June 2024].

4 Bellebono, J. 'Ladyboy', 2022. (no.1).

5 Barker, M. and Scheele, J. *Gender: A Graphic Guide*. London: Icon Books, 2019.

6 Mohanty, C. 'Under Western Eyes: Feminist Scholarship and Colonial Discourses'. *Feminist Review*, 30(1), 61-88, 1988. https://doi.org/10.1057/fr.1988.42.

7 Sage. @sagescrittore post on X.com (formerly Twitter.com), 25 October 2021.

8   Gedalof, I. 'Birth, belonging and migrant mothers: narratives of reproduction in feminist immigration studies'. *Feminist Review*, 93, 81–100, 2009. https://doi.org/10.1057/fr.2009.23.

9   Hall, J. *Shoulder to Shoulder: A Queer History of Solidarity, Coalition and Chaos.* London: Trapeze, 2024.

Chapter 5: Arts and Culture

1   McEvoy, C. 'Oscar Frontrunner Ke Huy Quan Had Quit Acting for Good. *Crazy Rich Asians* Brought Him Back'. Biography.com, 2023. Available at: https://www.biography.com/actors/a43236892/how-crazy-rich-asians-inspired-ken-huy-quan-return-to-acting [accessed 5 June 2024].

2   Asseraf, A. @ArthurAsseraf post on X.com (formerly Twitter.com), 16 January 2023.

3   Lee, P. 'Sex, Death, and Empire: The Roots of Violence Against Asian Women'. *The Nation*, May 2022.

4   Shimizu, C.P. *The Hypersexuality of Race: Performing Asian/American Women on Screen and Scene.* Durham, North Carolina: Duke University Press, 2007.

5   Chung, T. 'The Transnational Vision of Miss Saigon: Performing the Orient in a Globalized World'. *MELUS*, 36(4):61–86, 2011. https://doi.org/10.1353/mel.2011.0063.

6   New Earth Theatre. 'A statement from the co-producers of WORTH'. New Earth Theatre [online]. Available at: https://www.newearththeatre.org.uk/news/sheffield-statement [accessed 10 July 2024].

7   Beats.org. 'Statement About Miss Saigon'. Beats.org [online]. Available at: https://wearebeatsorg.org.uk/blog/statement-about-miss-saigon [accessed 16 October 2024].

8   Sheffield Theatres. 'A statement about New Earth and Storyhouse's Production of WORTH'. Sheffield Theatres [online]. Available

at: https://www.sheffieldtheatres.co.uk/news/worth-statement [accessed 10 July 2024].

9 Paul, L. 'The 1975's Matty Healy Apologizes for Offending Ice Spice, But Not for Those Same Offensive Jokes'. *Rolling Stone*, 21 April 2023 Available at: https://www.rollingstone.com/music/music-news/the-1975-matty-healy-ice-spice-apology-1234721163/ [accessed 24 July 2024].

10 Reilly, N. 'Rina Sawayama Calls Out Labelmate Matty Healy at Glastonbury: "I've Had Enough"'. *Rolling Stone*, 25 June 2023. Available at: https://www.rollingstone.com/music/music-news/rina-sawayama-matty-healy-glastonbury-1234777826/ [accessed 24 September 2024]; Beaumont-Thomas, B. ' "I've had enough": pop star Rina Sawayama criticises comments by labelmate Matty Healy'. *Guardian*, 24 June 2023. Available at https://www.theguardian.com/music/2023/jun/24/ive-had-enough-pop-star-rina-sawayama-criticises-comments-by-labelmate-matty-healy [accessed 24 September 2024].

11 Sawayama, R. @rinasawayama post on X.com (formerly Twitter.com), 24 February 2021.

12 Horwell, V. 'Jan Morris obituary'. *Guardian*, 2020. Available at: https://www.theguardian.com/books/2020/nov/20/jan-morris-obituary [accessed 21 May 2024].

13 Morris, J. *Hong Kong: Epilogue to an Empire*. New York City: Vintage Books, 1997.

14 Hampton, M. *Hong Kong and British Culture, 1945–97*. Manchester: Manchester University Press, 2015.

15 Pin, C. *Wandering Souls*. London: HarperCollins Publishers, 2023.

Chapter 6: Food

1 Sutton, D. and Masing A.S. 'A Taste of Home', *Taste of Place (Whetstone Radio Collective)* podcast, October 2022.

2   The Ivy Asia Chelsea. @theivyasiachelsea post on Instagram.com, 8 August 2021.

3   Armitage-Mattin, P. @chefphilli post on Instagram.com, 29 November 2020; Armitage-Mattin, P. cited in Breen, K. 'MasterChef contestant faces backlash for calling Asian food "dirty"'. Today.com [online], 1 December 2020. Available at: https://www.today.com/food/masterchef-contestant-faces-backlash-calling-asian-food-dirty-t202082 [accessed 25 July 2024].

4   Gordon Ramsay Restaurants, cited in Perraudin, F. 'Gordon Ramsay defends new restaurant in cultural appropriation row'. *Guardian*, 24 April 2019. Available at: https://www.theguardian.com/food/2019/apr/14/gordon-ramsay-defends-lucky-cat [accessed 25 July 2024].

5   Kambhu, D. Keynote speech at Food on the Edge symposium. Galway: 2019.

6   hooks, b. 'Eating the Other: Desire and Resistance' in *Black Looks: Race and Representation, Second Edition.* London: Routledge, 2014.

7   Freedman, P. *Out of the East: Spices and the Medieval Imagination.* New Haven, Connecticut: Yale University Press, 2009.

8   Walker, K. and Nesbitt, M. *Just the Tonic: A Natural History of Tonic Water.* London: Kew Publishing, 2019.

9   Tsang, S. *A Modern History of Hong Kong: 1841–1997.* London: Bloomsbury Academic, 2019.

10 Ibid.

11 Dove, M.R. *The Banana Tree at the Gate: A History of Marginal Peoples and Global Markets in Borneo.* New Haven, Connecticut: Yale University Press, 2011.

12 Ibid.

13 Makalintal, B. 'Great! AI Can Generate All the Diaspora Food Writing Tropes'. Eater, 2022. Available at: https://www.eater.com/23500787/openai-chatgpt-ai-chatbot-generates-diaspora-food-writing-tropes-stinky-lunchbox-moment [accessed 21 May 2024].

14 Stephanie, R. 'Spoons supper club founder Rahel Stephanie on

Indonesian food in the UK'. CODE, 2022. Available at: https://www.codehospitality.co.uk/industry_insights/spoons-founder-rahel-stephanie-on-indonesian-food-in-the-uk/ [accessed 4 June 2024].

Conclusion: Hidden Faces

1 'Pathe Reporter Meets (1948)'. YouTube, uploaded by British Pathé. 2014. Available at: https://youtu.be/QDH4IBeZF-M?si=f31cAoMQJXZarfRM [accessed 21 May 2024].
2 Quanch, G. 'Hackney's Pho Mile and Its History of Resistance'. *Huck*, 2022. Available at: https://www.huckmag.com/article/the-radical-legacy-of-hackneys-pho-mile [accessed 21 May 2024].
3 Dailly, M. @madevidailly post on X.com (formerly Twitter.com), 18 July 2022.
4 Masing, J.J. 'The Coming of the Gods: A Study of an Invocatory Chant (Timang Gawai Amat) of the Iban of the Baleh River Region of Sarawak'. Canberra: Australian National University, 1981.

Acknowledgements

I love reading acknowledgements because I love to see who the writer had around them, their backup singers and fellow bandmates. Writing a book is a group effort – it truly does take a village – and I am forever grateful for all those who have supported me in this wild ride.

It is a book I have been writing my whole life in so many ways, and with that comes the baggage of wanting to say so much, of having so many emotions, so much pain and joy, plus wanting to include all the people I have ever spoken to! I cannot begin to thank Maddy Price, my editor, who had the patience and care to wrangle all these things into a coherent manuscript – whose delicate and thoughtful editing coaxed my voice out. And, most importantly – believed I could even write this book! Thank you also to editors Kate Moreton and Nina Sandelson, and the whole Weidenfeld & Nicolson team, including Susie Bertinshaw, brilliant sub-editor Suyin Haynes, Steve Leard for the beautiful cover, and Minjoo Ham for wonderful the typeface.

This journey of writing and dreaming of books would be impossible without my agent Holly Faulks. Holly

contacted me off the back of a tweet where I said I wanted
to write a memoir based on durians, during a pandemic
lockdown – I then spilled out all the things I wanted to
do and write (durian memoir tbc, lol). Holly is constantly
championing me, taking time to listen to my concerns,
to always read my work, and nod sagely at the slightly
madcap ideas. Writing is a very lonely task and to be from
a marginalised identity can further add to that, but to be
cared for, as Holly makes me feel, is invaluable. Thank
you, Holly!

When writing and researching colonialism, race and
identity, it can be a sad and angry world to exist in and
ensuring joy is also present is hugely important. For me,
work and life blend into one and my professional network
of incredible women, who are now also my dear friends,
is a great source of joy (we still concern ourselves with
colonialism, race and identity but more as a group effort!).
Cheese mag brings me an abundance of joy, thank you,
Holly Catford and Apoorva Sripathi for making this wild
dream a reality. Frankie Reddin for the ride-or-die world-
domination vibes, and for always saying we're on holiday
when actually it's work – joy, joy, joy! And Chloe-Rose
Crabtree for the meals, the shoulder to lean/cry/laugh on
when life has been too tough to do it on my own; your
friendship is home.

This book could not exist without the people who
spoke to me so honestly. In particular Vera Chok, Jenny
Lau and Safiah Durrah Hashim – who over the years I
have had such deep conversations with, who have offered

ACKNOWLEDGEMENTS

me a space to question myself and each other. Navigating
this space is complex and difficult. Thank you, Jenny, for
always taking the time to meander around thoughts, for
challenging me, for listening to my frustrations and anger,
but also for making me laugh! Goddamn it, we are really
fucking funny!

Veranna 4 eva – MEEEP!

And, of course, thank you to all in the book – I am
so grateful for your time and generosity. Plus those who
spoke to me but whose words did not make the final
draft – I hope you see your voices imprinted throughout
– thank you!

I wouldn't be the writer and researcher I am today
without my PhD supervisors, Irene Gedalof and Lucy
Richardson. I owe them so much, including how to be
Iban – they pushed me to question my heritage, to search,
to research, to interrogate my insider-ness but also my
outsider-ness, to be critical and to be proud, to value my
voice.

To my daily podcast listener of one – Emma Hughes,
thank you! Long live the voice note. For reading this
book, in various drafts; for taking every little concern and
treating them with gravitas (that they didn't always need).
For all my friends who have supported me during this
time and always – James Hansen, Catherine Kirk, Zoe
Cooper, Miranda York, Oli, Mat, Phoebe, Julia, David
(and all your bold commissioning), Claire and Jake who
read various chapters, the Invite Only gang, the 'where's
Lottie?' group chat: Clare, Charlotte, Amy, Cheryl, Emily,

Mandy. All the WhatsApp groups tbh. Mandy and Yao, and the whole Sambal Shiok team. The wonderful writing, food and drinks community – I <3 you. Coco and Jonah – animals, a writer's greatest companions.

And, of course, my family, without whom it would be impossible. My siblings, who are the funniest people I know – Ashley, Emma, Karen and Rachel, whose TikTok videos and bearing with me her whole life is truly appreciated. My lovely stepmother, Maria. My wonderful stepdad, Grant. Flo. Nicolás Luyoh and Samuel Awan (you're almost as funny as your uncle and aunts). Jean-Baptiste, who quite literally ensured I had a roof over my head and food in my belly, as well as making sure I had fun holidays and fancy meals during this book writing process, as well as all the times (PhD included) that I was deep in (unpaid) research without which this book would not exist.

Mum – who taught me to be me, and allowed me to be brave in myself. Who taught me to celebrate, and to be sensible and work hard. Thank you for everything.

Dad – I can't believe you won't read this book. I can imagine so clearly what bits you would underline and, if I was sitting next to you, which bits you would half turn to me, pat my shoulder and peer over your glasses in a knowing look. You are my inspiration.